D0485939

DON'T
MESS
WITH
THE
LOGO

FT Prentice Hall

FINANCIAL TIMES

In an increasingly competitive world, we believe it is quality of thinking that will give you the edge – an idea that opens new doors, a technique that solves a problem, or an insight that simply makes sense of it all. The more you know, the smarter and faster you can go.

That is why we work with the best minds in business and finance to bring cutting-edge thinking and best learning practice to a global market.

Under a range of leading imprints, including *Financial Times Prentice Hall*, we create world-class print publications and electronic products bringing our readers knowledge, skills and understanding, which can be applied whether studying or at work.

To find out more about Pearson Education publications, or tell us about the books you would like to find, you can visit us at **www.pearsoned.co.uk.**

PEARSON
Education

DON'T MESS WITH THE LOGO

THE STRAIGHT TALKER'S BIBLE OF BRANDING

Jon Edge & Andy Milligan

FT Prentice Hall
FINANCIAL TIMES

An imprint of **Pearson Education**

Harlow, England • London • New York • Boston • San Francisco • Toronto • Sydney • Singapore • Hong Kong
Tokyo • Seoul • Taipei • New Delhi • Cape Town • Madrid • Mexico City • Amsterdam • Munich • Paris • Milan

PEARSON EDUCATION LIMITED

Edinburgh Gate
Harlow CM20 2JE
Tel: +44 (0)1279 623623
Fax: +44 (0)1279 431059

Website: www.business-minds.com

First published in Great Britain in 2009

© Pearson Education Limited 2009

The right of Jon Edge and Andy Milligan to be identified as authors of this work has been asserted by them in accordance with the Copyright, Designs and Patents Act 1988.

ISBN: 978-0-273-71420-0

British Library Cataloguing in Publication Data
A CIP catalogue record for this book can be obtained from the British Library.

Library of Congress Cataloging-in-Publication Data

Edge, Jon.
  Don't mess with the logo : the straight talker's bible of branding / Jon Edge & Andy Milligan.
    p. cm.
  Includes bibliographical references and index.
  ISBN 978-0-273-71420-0 (pbk. : alk. paper) 1. Branding (Marketing) 2. Brand name products. 3. Advertising--Brand name products. I. Milligan, Andy. II. Title.
  HF5415.1255.E34 2009
  658.8'27--dc22

                                                        2009016489

10 9 8 7 6 5 4 3 2
13 12 11 10 09

Typeset by 30
Printed by Ashford Colour Press Ltd., Gosport

The Publishers' policy is to use paper manufactured from sustainable forests.

This book is dedicated by Andy to Susannah, Ted and Frank
And by Jon to his beautiful mum, and brilliant dad and brothers

CONTENTS

THANKS

Many people are involved in the production of a book like this. Too many to thank individually. But we have tried. So here goes.

Thanks to Liz Gooster for painstaking patience and support. Richard Stagg for his support in the initial stages of the project. Our respective families for being our families. Doug Hamilton of WHAM for letting Jon write the book. Chris Cowpe and David Kean of The Caffeine Partnership for reading the manuscript. The designers, typesetters and booksellers.

And thanks from Andy to John Murphy and Tom Blackett without whom I would never have discovered the "funderful" world of brands.

INTRODUCTION

"Make everything as simple as possible, but not simpler." Albert Einstein

Hello™. Thanks for buying our book. There's a funny story behind its title. Originally, it was going to be called Don't F*** With The Logo. Why? Well, for three reasons:

1 It's what a CEO once said to a consultancy when they were asked to review his brand identity. "You can do anything you want with the brand, just don't f*** with the logo". We think it nicely sums up the confusion and lack of understanding a lot of people still have about those two words: brand and logo.

2 People obsess with the image and icons of brands as if it would only need a change of logo or a new ad campaign and all would be well. In fact, it is almost always the experience that we have of brands that determines what we think of them. So don't bother messing around with the logo, do something about the experience

3 It's different from other book titles and captures the spirit of how we want this book to be read. Differentiation and personality are the essentials of brands and we hope you will find this book different and with its own feisty little personality.

But here's a lesson in co-branding. The brand folks at FT, our publisher, said they didn't want their brand to be associated with swearing as it didn't fit their image. Well they are the publishing brand so that's fair. Of course, we're the author brand and we wanted this book to sell like hotcakes and thought the title would dramatically help that cause. Let's face it, 'f***' kinda leaps off the book shelf at you, demanding to be bought. Before you know it you've picked up the book and headed to the cash till without pausing to think why. That's our theory. But 'no' said the FT. Their brand is not a sweary brand. And as we said, it's their brand and that's fair. So we stuck the word 'mess' over the word 'f***' like a Band-Aid™. And everyone's happy. So you see, in a business world of increasing joint ventures, where different partners come together each with its own brand objectives, you have to learn to compromise without sacrificing what is important to you. There, we've given you a real life lesson in branding already and you're only on the first page.

So who are you? Whether you're a future-proof CEO that likes to stay ahead of the curve; a marketing director or marketing manager 12 months into your job and currently thinking about something smart to say at your next interview; a student; a consultant; a designer; a consultant that used to be a designer; a creative director, a design director, a part-time actor/model and media receptionist; an account person that has got kerning[1] and now you're taking it to the next level; a head of something; a rookie; just like having lots of books on design or branding; want to know how to sound insightful by using words like zeitgeist, paradigm shift or haberdashery; work for

---

[1] Kerning is the technical term printers use for the spacing between letters in any printed page (see, you'll learn interesting stuff like this in this book).

somewhere that says on the web they do branding; are dating someone that is in branding and you want to impress them; are desperately trying to see if we've nicked any of the ideas you were discussing in the queue for the T-bar; want to see if we mentioned you in the thanks bit; think swearing in books is big and clever; are having a break from BookFaced, YouSpace, MyTube or whatever social networking sites exist; are in the dark or down with the kids – then this book is for you.

If, however, you're an anal-retentive, strategy-obsessed, two-by-two-matrix-wielding, business-theory-crazed, model-mad nerd head expecting to find more charts and models to put into your PowerPoint brand onion presentations, then you probably won't like this book and you certainly won't appreciate, or even be ready for, such genius as the brand fox. If you fear you might be one of these, please buy the book (so you can say you have it) but don't read it – it will probably break you out in a rash. Oh all right, we have put some models and charts in here to appeal to you and, you never know, you might find some things in here that you can use and with which you agree.

We think brands are great concepts and, if delivered with style, authenticity and a genuine respect for what they stand for and whom they serve, then they are probably the most fun you can have in business. More importantly they are the best way we know of making long-term money for businesses. We also think that they are the simplest concept in business and have been plastered with lashings of needlessly complex bullsh*t.

This book gives simple, practical advice on all the things you need to consider in building a brand. Each subject we deal with is probably worth a book on its own – in fact, come to think of it, there are whole books on those subjects. This book aims to distil the key issues on those subjects to make it easy for you to get an understanding of why they're important, what they are about and what you need to remember about them. And we hope we've done it in a way that is fun and useful.

This book is meant to be read in small bite-size bits. On a plane. On a train. On a toilet. Whenever you want to dip into a chapter that seems most relevant to you. But if you want to read it in one go, then turn your Digibox off, unplug your Crackberry, go and make yourself a nice cup of tea or coffee. Feel the force and get in the zone. In a minute we're going to take you on a journey down brand boulevard, do a U-turn in logo cul-de-sac before putting the hammer down in the fast lane of brand-enlightenment. Ready? Now read on.

A rose by any other name would smell as sweet.

William Shakespeare, *Romeo & Juliet*

A hamburger by any other name costs twice as much.

Groucho Marx (attributed)

WHY YOU NEED TO BE ON THE BRANDWAGON

A brief (we promise) history of brands and why they're so valuable

Brand	*n.* a particular product; particular kind of variety; identifying mark burnt on to the skin of an animal; *v.* mark with a brand; denounce as being.
Brand new	*adj.* absolutely new.
Brandish	*v.* wave (a weapon, etc.) in a threatening way.
Brandy	*n.* pl.-**dies** alcoholic spirit distilled from wine.

Brand, brand, brand. Everybody keeps using the word. What do we know about brands? Brands are logos, aren't they? Brands tell you to do things, don't they? Brands are bad, brands are good, brands are people. Everything and everyone seems to be a brand these days. Celebrities are the new brands – *Big Brother* is perhaps the best example of how ridiculous this concept has become – like modern art, it's apparently enough to proclaim someone a celebrity, get them on the TV for a bit, and they become a papparazzi-snapped self-fullfilling prophecy of fame. A household celebrity DJ in the UK, Jonathan King, who was convicted of a sex offence, proclaimed, "Jonathan King was not in fact real, but a brand." Every car salesman you meet now talks more about "the brand" than the car. But what does it all really mean? Don't they just mean logos? It's confusing, isn't it, when you're trying to work out where all your brand value has gone? Disappeared down the back of the brand sofa, probably.

You could rescue it if it's a master brand, just sort out the brand equity and re-align your brand architecture to create a brand-space for the sub-brands. You probably need some brand strategy and the brand, the real brand (i.e. the brand marque or brand icon) will need a brand refresh and some brand guardianship from the brand team, internally and externally brand focused to be brand evangelists using brand elements as laid out in the brand guidelines, informed by the brand values, brand personality, brand vision, brand mission and brand mantra from the brand aura – derived from the brand spirit of the brand book. Meanwhile no wonder Angry of Tunbridge Wells is spitting his Tesco Finest coffee over his IKEA sofa watching Sky News – as another brand spokesman explains why a logo that looks like something his five-year-old could draw has cost a million-billion-skillion pounds. Is it really branding that is causing all this upset, making innocent™ people spit out their drinks and melting the polar ice caps? Why are we so obsessed with them? And why does what the so-called brand experts we hear on TV, the radio or in the press say often make so little sense to us? Maybe it's because they need to make it seem too difficult for the average person to understand in order to justify their fees. So let's start by setting the record straight on when all this brand brouhaha began, why they are worth that million-skillion pounds and why we're obssessed with them.

How it all began

We'll skip all the stuff about the Norse word *brandr* (to burn) being the origination of our word brand; also we'll miss out how cattle were branded to show who owned them until Maverick came up with the world's first anti-brand (Naomi Klein would have loved him) by claiming all unbranded cattle were his. We'll deftly pass over the rise of the commercial mark in trade, and the law established to protect the rights of both consumer and proprietor against unscrupulous third parties. Thus, sadly, we'll also ignore Manet's famous painting *A bar at the Folies-Bergère* (1882) featuring the world's first registered trademark, the Bass Ale Red Triangle. (Here's a picture of it.)

The Samuel Courtauld Trust, The Courtauld Gallery, London

By the way, if anyone asks you, "What rights does a trademark protect for consumers?", tell them: the right to know they are purchasing bona fide goods – and since people literally consume most of those goods – e.g. Bass Ale – knowing they have come from a safe and trusted source is an important, possibly life-saving, right. There are other books around that do all that and we've given you a bibliography of these on page 208. Anyway, though it's interesting, all that history stuff is largely irrelevant.

What matters is that – just like sex, which for the British poet Philip Larkin famously began in 1963 – brands for us (Jon and Andy) began in 1988, somewhere around the time that Rank Hovis McDougall (RHM), one of the UK's leading branded goods businesses, fought off a hostile acquisition from the Australian firm Goodman Fielder Watts (GFW) by the ingenious strategem of having all its brands (e.g. Hovis bread, Saxa salt, Bisto gravy) valued financially and including their value on its balance sheet. This ramped up the value of RHM dramatically and beyond the price that GFW was prepared to pay. The value of brands had saved the day for RHM!

Of course, like sex before 1963, brands had been around long before 1988. They had been ticking along very nicely but were mostly the responsibility of marketing men and advertising chaps. And most brands were branded goods businesses, i.e. a product people could touch and then consume off the shelf. But following the RHM valuation, brands became recognised as corporate assets and slowly but surely CEOs, CFOs, investors and analysts became interested in them. And realised they had to be treated seriously.

Then during the 1990s a number of big changes happened in the business world that ratcheted up the importance of brands. These included:

- the deregulation and privatisation of markets and capital (until September 2008 most people thought this was a good thing: now you don't need to be an established bank to sell financial services – ask Virgin – and you can sell anything anywhere under the same name – ask Virgin, again);
- the extension of trademark protection to services as well as manufactured goods (that means McDonald's became a brand technically!);

- the outsourcing of manufacturing to countries with cheaper labour (yep, Naomi Klein covered that in *No Logo*) leading to the rise of the marketing and sales company, e.g. Nike, which didn't manufacture anything but built markets for its brands;
- the growth of an affluent middle class globally with more money than time (did you know that over a billion people have been added to the world's middle classes since 1990?);
- the deline of trust in political and cultural institutions and the rise in the power of consumers;
- the attendant growth of the service economy, the rise of global media and global media buying (once Ted Turner and Rupert Murdoch had shown that news and entertainment could be consumed everywhere in the same way);
- the rise of the concept of shareholder value and the principle of Economic Value Added (i.e. that businesses could make more money by owning intangible assets, e.g. patents and trademarks, than tangible ones, e.g. factories).

In this brave new borderless world, brands captured people's imaginations because, unlike the manufactured products they sold, they could slip easily across frontiers of all kinds, including the most important of all, the limitless frontier of the consumer's mind. Consumers recognised brands and they trusted them – politicians let you down, Volkswagen cars didn't. They liked them because there was something with which they could identify, something that connected with them, something they could enjoy or aspire to. They were cool or they were not cool but either way someone loved them. And daily they gave people an illusory feeling of power and control. Heck, life might be hard work and boring, my future might be uncertain, my government doesn't care about me and the climate is beyond my control but I can *choose* to buy or not to buy that can of Coca-Cola™. And what's more we could all have real fun with them on a daily basis. Before BA could say "vomit comet", prime ministers started putting handkerchiefs over branded tailfins. Kids got happy-slapped in the face at school while drinking Tango orange drinks and pretty soon we'd ditched the BT piper and rejected the Hutchison Rabbit and were going crazy for Orange phones. Suddenly in advertising, brands started telling the public about "What they believed in". A raft of new names and logos came out, consultants started seeking a global outlook and local insight, designers were having a f***ing laugh and branding was here to stay and was on the boardroom agenda.

And then what took brands into another sphere of influence altogether was the internet. First it was the dot.com boom. That showed the world that you did not necessarily need to sell anything, hell you did not even need to have any customers – and a sustainable, profitable business model was so, like, yesterday, dude! All you needed was a brand and you could command millions. Lawyers were called in to register and protect ridiculous names like boo.com or boo.hoo.com or maybe whatabooboo.com and businesses were sold for fortunes on the basis of a business plan written on the back of a software manual guaranteed by a globally protected trademark. Even though dot.com dot.bombed, what it left behind was the realisation that a brand gave you a valuable range of options and the internet gave you powerful ways of using those options to weave your way into people's lives.

Why are brands so important?

Now why is this brief history important? Simply because it tells us the reasons – and these are the only reasons – why you need a brand. You need a brand because:

1 people (that includes you and us) believe they stand for something they value personally and so are prepared to pay more for them or to buy them repeatedly;

2 (therefore) you make more money with one than without one;

3 they legally protect your rights to make that money – they protect your idea not just your product and so stop other people making money at your expense;

4 they allow you to launch new products and services, etc. under that idea more cheaply (i.e. so you can make even more money);

5 they act as a "barrier to entry" to competition in your market (you could make a cola drink, sure, but are you really going to be able to take on Coca-Cola™?);

6 they help attract and retain people who want to work for you – who help you make money;

7 in order to make that money continuously, they force you to deliver consistently a differentiated promise of value to your customers;

8 chicks dig 'em and guys think they're cool.

That's all. Every other reason anyone gives you for needing a brand falls under one or another of those. Go on, you can try the game at home: think of a reason for being in business and it will fall under one of those reasons for having a brand. Doing something you like? Having a clear corporate strategy? See reasons 1, 4 and 6. Making money? Shareholder value? Reasons 1, 2 and 4. Making a difference? Corporate social responsibility? 5 and 6, and even 7. And so on.

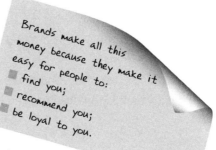

Brands make all this money because they make it easy for people to:
- find you;
- recommend you;
- be loyal to you.

And it is all about making money. And that is a good thing. Profits are proof of success. Don't get confused when someone tells you charities are brands. Charities have brands. The charity exists to make a difference in the world; its brand exists to raise the money to do that. People are not brands, although brands can be people. David Beckham is a human being not a brand but there is a brand called David Beckham™ which makes a lot of money.

Brands do not change the world, heal the poor, cure the sick or act as ambassadors of international peace. People do all that but brands are one of the best tools we have created to help them achieve that. Because they make money. How much money? Well, so much that consultancies have even set up rival league tables to tell us how much brands are worth.

Who's right? Who cares? The point is everyone now understands that brands = long-term money. And long-term money gives you the power to change things. That's why we're obsessed with them. And that is why you have to be on the brandwagon.

RANK	BRAND	BRAND VALUE ($M)	BRAND VALUE CHANGE
1	Google	86,057	30%
2	GE (General Electric)	71,379	15%
3	Microsoft	70,887	29%
4	Coca-Cola	58,208	17%
5	China Mobile	57,225	39%
6	IBM	55,335	65%
7	Apple	55,206	123%
8	McDonald's	49,499	49%
9	Nokia	43,975	39%
10	Marlboro	37,324	–5%

Brand League Table 2008

RANK	BRAND	BRAND VALUE ($M)	BRAND VALUE CHANGE
1	Coca-Cola	66,667	2%
2	IBM	59,031	3%
3	Microsoft	59,007	1%
4	GE (General Electric)	53,086	3%
5	Nokia	57,225	7%
6	Toyota	34,050	6%
7	Intel	31,261	1%
8	McDonald's	31,049	6%
9	Disney	29,251	0%
10	Google	25,590	43%

BusinessWeek Global Brands Scoreboard 2008

A product is made in a factory. A brand is created in the mind.

Stephen King (no, not *that* Stephen King)

SO WHAT IS A BRAND?

*2

Here is another game you can play at home. Google™ the word "brand" and see how many mentions you get. Now Google™ the phrase "what is a brand?" and see how many threads come up. Now read one or two of those threads and you will not get a single, consistent definition of a brand. Why is this? Partly because there is no global body of branding – as there is of, say, accounting – that has agreed on one, partly because the people involved in the brand definition process come from so many different backgrounds (advertising, marketing, design, management consulting, research) that they can't reach a common vocabulary, and partly because we're too lazy and it suits the charlatan in us all not to have one. But also because there are two different technical areas in which the word brand is defined: a legal one and a marketing one.

Legally, a brand means a trademark, which distinguishes the goods or services of one supplier from another. In marketing terms, a brand means a specific promise of value, which the business must deliver to its customer. And there is even an economic definition now: a brand is a corporate asset that generates specific and protectable revenues (as we saw in those league tables in Chapter 1).

What is a brand?

A brand is best described as the sum of all the parts of a business, product or organisation. Everything you do, everything you say is captured in your trademark.

So, although agencies often refer to the logo or advert (or probably whatever bit they can sell you) as "the brand" –

actually, it's not one single thing. Successful brands get this and you'll see that they follow this holistic view. It's about making sure that everything matters and the whole is what is really your brand. So, there you have your answer: brand is the sum of the parts of a business, product or thing.

brand is the sum of the parts of a business, product or thing.

Now, let's not have to keep explaining this one, otherwise it'll get a bit irritating. Just in case you didn't get it – it's not one thing – so it's not the logo, it's not a wordmarque, logotype, icon or mascot – it's not even an avatar either (although avatars are cool). It's not a gas, it's not electricity, it's not a myth, a typeface, it's not a trademark, a sound, an ad, a strapline, a space, a label or a website. All of these things can be part of the brand, but it's what people perceive about all these components that makes it a brand. In fact it's probably time for our first diagram.

Here's a formula that's often used to describe a brand:

$P + I = B$

That's Product + Image = Brand

Product (what you make in the factory) + Image (what you make in the mind) = Brand (what people think about it)

That worked well for soap powders, toothpaste, etc.

Flouride toothpaste + fresh-breath confidence = Colgate

E × E × E = B
Essence × Expression ×
Experience = Brand

But it's trickier now that everything is a brand and we can experience the same brand in a dozen different ways (like Virgin or Disney, for example) and each experience multiplies our perceptions of that brand.

We think it's now this:

E × E × E = B

Essence × Expression × Experience = Brand

Essence (what you stand for) × Expression (how you communicate it) × Experience (what you actually make or provide) = Brand (what people think of you)

And that works for everything.

Magic × colour, fun, no cynicism × family entertainment = Disney

It's normally round about here in the company PowerPoint that the words with z or the ideation™ ownership techniques would kick in. But we don't want any of those, we want to keep it simple and no simpler.

The simplest way to break down the brands that we come into contact with is: product, behaviour, environment and communication. Product – as in things, tangible stuff – fast-moving consumer goods (FMCG) in the old days but anything you sell these days, so services fit in here as well. Product is, for example, the coke drink and all its variations; it's Apple's iPod MP3 player, the Porsche 911 car, the Microsoft operating system.

The simplest way to break down the brands that we come into contact with is: product, behaviour, environment and communication.

Behaviours are how the brand acts – as in the people that work for the brand – this means not just answering the phone "on-brand" but your people actually believing in what they do, contributing and growing the brand. FedEx famously has staff that will get the job done, even if that means booking a helicopter on their credit card to get to the top of a mountain. Environment means everything from an HQ to a shop, an exhibition stand, the inside of a plane; not just walls to stick graphics on but spaces, real or virtual (i.e. websites, etc.) – future facing eh? And, finally, communication, the sexiest bit (often) because it's often the most visible and the reason why everyone normally focuses on the "logo" as it's easy to latch onto how things look. If you're really funny and you want to get on with strategy consultants or accounts people in agencies, you could also refer to this bit as "colouring in". They never get tired of that joke. It's a classic. But seriously, folks, these days in the 21st century, communication alone is far more than words or pictures; digital progress has given us aural expression, sonics, film and all that jazz.

If a brand is the sum of everything, then those are all the things you need to create the brand. Stephen King – the legendary planner of the advertising world, not the novelist – points out that a trademark acts as a promise of an experience to people. All you have to do is stay true to the promise that your distinctive trademark makes.

It really is that simple.

Apple understands that. Coca-Cola understands that. Nike understands that. The folks at Procter & Gamble, Unilever or at Harley-Davidson, Amazon or Virgin, they all understand that. Understanding that great brands get 100 per cent of everything right is key to understanding branding. As Chris Bangle, the former Head of Design at BMW said: "We make mobile art, not automobiles." So as we say, "Don't mess about with logos, or try to copy the look but not the quality or innovation of brands like Apple or BMW. You'll fail."

And this works for any kind of brand. Is Rubik's Cube a brand? Yes. Of course it is. Not just a trademark but a whole experience.

David Hedley Jones works for Seven Towns, which owns the Rubik's licence. He said:

> In 1980, the Rubik's Cube was launched on an unsuspecting world with a Hollywood party hosted by the 'other' famous Hungarian Zsa Zsa Gabor. Little did anyone know it would become

the world's biggest-selling puzzle. Today it looks the same, it works the same and it's still incredibly popular. So iconic did the puzzle become that it earned a place in New York's Museum of Modern Art, and its own entry in the *Oxford English Dictionary*; not to mention worldwide sales exceeding 300 million copies. Rubik's Cube has featured in major movies and ad campaigns, been used as a generic platform for mind puzzles in general, generated huge sales of T-shirts and apparel, been used as an iconic image for lottery games and scratch cards and, along with the brand's other 3D twisting puzzles, still generates a huge amount of public interest, recognition and affection.

There you are: a quirky, colourful geometrical puzzle became a global brand because it has a whole "experience" surrounding it.

How to build a brand

And what do we learn from these brands? The six rules that you have to follow to build a great brand are:

1 Develop a strategy that is clear and easy to understand.

2 Create a simple brand architecture that links the different things you do in a way that makes sense to your consumers.

3 Develop a distinctive brand identity that you can protect by law.

4 Ensure you have a consistent and iconic customer experience across your products, the places in which you sell them and the people that work for you.

5 Set up dedicated brand management and measurement structures and processes.

6 Don't f*** (sorry, mess) with the logo.

So let's start looking at those rules in more detail, always remembering that rules are for the obedience of fools and the guidance of wise men.

But, before we do, just repeat this sentence over and over to yourself:

"If I stay true to my promise, I'll make money."

Go on.

> "If I stay true to my promise, I'll make money."
> "If I stay true to my promise, I'll make money."
> "If I stay true to my promise, I'll make money."
> "If I stay true to my promise, I'll make money."

Do it every day.

"Everything you say, everything you do." That's what a brand is, then.

"

In preparing for battle I have always found that plans are useless, but planning is indispensable.

Dwight D. Eisenhower or General Patton (or maybe it was both, no one seems sure)

"

WHAT IS
BRAND
STRATEGY?

*3

Strategy is possibly the most overused and often misapplied word in business. And brand strategy is particularly overused. All strategy means is having a plan. In brand building, you need to distinguish between many types of strategy, of which the most common are as follows:

Corporate or business strategy which means what the business intends to do and how it intends to do it (of which brand strategy should be a part).

Marketing strategy which is how to segment your customers and develop, launch, communicate, distribute and deliver offers for them – closely aligned to brand strategy and often marketing strategy is driven by brand strategy but sometimes (if you are Procter & Gamble, say) marketing strategy may drive brand strategy.

Media strategy which is about how and where and how much you are going to invest in exposing your brand to customers (which medium is best suited to your needs: TV, Web, viral marketing? etc.). Media strategy must be driven by your brand strategy.

Creative strategy which is really the idea behind the creative execution of your advertising or visual identity, etc., etc. This again must be driven by your brand strategy.

And then there is *brand strategy* which is the plan you develop for building your brand. And that is what we are interested in in this book.

What is a good brand strategy?

A good brand strategy answers the following five questions simply and clearly:

1 What will we stand for?
A clear idea of who the brand is targeted at and what it offers to those customers that is different from competitors.

2 How many sub-brands do we need?
A clear idea of how many brands or sub-brands it will own (we call this brand architecture).

3 What will our brand identity be?
A clear brief for its name, logo, etc.

4 How are we going to deliver this?
What are the promises it will make across product, people, communications and environments and how will they be delivered so that people believe it?

5 How will we know we've succeeded?
What will be the measures we will use to judge success?

Unfortunately, many people use the term "brand strategy" for any part of the brand-building process that requires strategic thinking and so it is easy to get confused. For example, an advertising agency may tell you they are developing your brand strategy when they are actually developing a strategy for your advertising. Or a design business might say they are developing your brand strategy when in fact they are developing the idea for your brand name and brand visual identity.

Brand model schmodel

Then, there is another problem. Strategic brand models. There are far too many of them. In the laudable attempt to make the brand strategy memorable, agencies and consultancies developed helpful little visual tools to present the content of the strategy visually. So we take all the components of the strategy and put them into a diagram that is the shape of a wheel. And that becomes a "brand wheel". Which makes sense. But then from there, somehow, people made this visual device the "strategic model" itself. And then this "model" became a proprietorial tool that different agencies or consultancies owned and used to show their expertise and point of difference. And, before you know it, people are wandering round the corridors of business asking, "have we got our brand wheel?" And there are hundreds of them: brand prisms, brand ladders, brand pyramids, brand houses, brand foundations, brand platforms, brand ripples (cast the idea onto the pond and see how the communications issues surround it like ripples) and brand onions. Yes, brand onions. Because, like an onion, you need to peel each layer of the brand before you get to the core.

We've roughly sketched some of the most common ones you'll come across so you can recognise them when you see them.

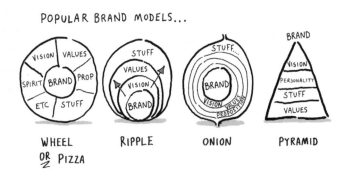

POPULAR BRAND MODELS...

WHEEL OR PIZZA   RIPPLE   ONION   PYRAMID

You see, you can become a brand spotter, tick them off when you see them and share them with other brand spotters: "hey, I saw a brand platform yesterday." "That's nothing, mate, I saw two brand onions and a brand wheel."

Daniel Keller, the Global Brand Strategy Director at Orange points out that brand models only get you so far; more important is the energy and conviction with which you communicate internally:

> The two key things that make a brand a successful organising principle in any business are a convincing story and lots of energy to get your people behind it. To keep things simple and your message consistent, it can help to summarise your story as a brand formula, brand key, onion, whatever suits your taste and needs. To make it heard and being applied, it's all down to the energy you invest into explaining and demonstrating it again and again. And again.

The brand fox

We don't really like conventional "brand onion" type diagrams – we think brand onions end in tears.

We've got our own model; we call it the brand fox. And that's a trademark as far as we are concerned so you can't use it. The following illustration shows how it works.

A fox is a great analogy for a brand as it's actually alive, and unpredictable. It's able to adapt and it can see in the dark. It also gets stuck in a unique way sometimes during copulation (think of AOL and Time Warner).

The similarities don't stop there. The idea is the heart, the central driving force. The head is communication – it speaks for the brand. The brain is the strategy part, thinking, reacting and informing the heart (idea). The tail is the behaviour – a reflection of the mood or desire of the brand. Nice and bushy. The coat is the environment, what surrounds it and presents the most obvious interactive experience (go on, stroke the brand). Its genitalia is the creative bit (obvious enough). Its tongue, the research input. Product is represented by its muscles (some are its best assets and others are in development). And we've put viral marketing on its back legs – we could put it anywhere because no one f***ing understands viral marketing anyway. So there you have it – that's how a brand works, as a fox. Don't put that in your PowerPoint™, it's ours – but do spread the legend, feel its power.

It's worth pointing out that the brand fox eats brand onions for breakfast, in fact he's had so many he doesn't even care for them any more, he thinks they are passé. In fact the brand fox is so cultured and hip he's post-brand-vegan.

Questions you should ask about your brand strategy

You don't have to be Gary Kasparov to realise that strategy simply means what you plan to do next. Brand strategy is the same – what will your brand do, change or become? So how do you know if you are getting good advice on brand strategy? Here are some of the questions you need to ask your agency or, if you are a CEO, your brand or marketing department:

1 How is this strategy going to help me meet my business objectives?

   Good answers:

   ■ Everyone in your market is talking about x, this talks about y (Nike v. Adidas).

   ■ There's nothing intrinsically new about this, it's the way we'll do it that's different (innocent smoothies).

   ■ No one has ever put x and y together before (e.g. the movie *Alien: Jaws in space*).

   ■ What is your primary objective beyond revenue? (Answering with a smart question can win some points!)

   Bad answers:

   ■ What do you mean, "business objectives"?

■ There's nothing different, we'll make our business out of copying what everyone has done (possible brownie points for refreshing honesty).

2 Why is this relevant to my customers and future customers and the people who work here?

Good answer:

■ Your target customers want x above everything else.

Bad answer:

■ This is what your competitor is talking about.

3 Can you explain this strategy in words of approximately one syllable that a person of average intelligence can understand?

Good answer:

■ Yes.

Bad answer:

■ It's not that simple.

4 Give me examples of what exactly this strategy might mean (in real life) for my business. And do you really think we can do this?

Good answer:

■ Here's what types of products we could develop. Here's what could be done in store, etc., etc.

Bad answer:

■ We can evolve the campaign over time.

5 Am I going to need a new strategy in five years' time?

Good answer:

■ No.

Bad answer:

■ Change is the only constant.

Red Bull has a great brand strategy. It was different because no one had put together the idea of an energy drink with a drink for clubbers before. It was relevant because there were a growing number of youngsters who were clubbing until dawn or doing weird extreme sports all day and they needed energy in an easy, fun way. It gave people wings. Red Bull entered each market by targeting clubbers and extreme sports or "cool sports" enthusiasts. In the USA, for example, they hired kids to distribute and demand it in some states so promoting it "virally" to give it a brand buzz as well as a buzz buzz. And they didn't really need a new strategy in five years' time, they waited until they had enough critical mass and then supported their grass-roots campaign with TV ads primarily intended to reinforce product perceptions rather than create awareness.

Then take something like Pepsi Clear. We can almost guarantee that that brand had a proper brand model applied to it, but who really wanted clear cola?

There you are, Red Bull has wings but we don't think it has an onion. Remember all brand onions will end in tears – either that or the brand fox will eat them.

Only connect.

E. M. Forster

THE HOUSE THAT BRAND BUILT

Positioning and brand architecture

Real-life anecdote No. 1

A friend of ours got a call the other day from someone working for a large financial services company – we won't tell you whom but it is one of those ones everyone's heard of. And the person calling says:

"I wonder if you could come in and help us. You know we developed a new positioning for ourselves last year that the agency came up with and that worked well but the marketing director has left now and we've got the agency working on a new positioning for us."

"Umm…right? And how could I help?" says our friend.

"Well we think the positionings, well really they're propositions which we are working on, need to be integrated into our brand more."

"Integrated into your brand?"

"Yes, into our brand essence."

"The brand essence?"

"Yeah, you know really, the DNA of the brand."

"And what is your brand essence?"

"Well, we don't really know, sort of integrity, I think, but that's what we'd like you to help us define."

"Umm … OK."

"Can you, or anyone else, like, help us?"

"Well, how much time do you have for this?"

"Oh, three days."

"Three days? Exactly three days?"

"Yes."

"OK. I'll see what I can do [pauses]. Oh, I'm sorry. I can't. I'll see if I can find someone who can."

Yes, conversations like these really do happen. But it got us thinking. Does anybody know any more what a positioning is? And what a proposition is? And as for brand essence …

Brand essence? Brand DNA? Brand proposition? Brand promise? Brand soul? Brand heart? Brand philosophy? Brand metempsychosis?[1] We've heard them all. They are all attempts to suggest that there is something fundamental beyond the extrinsic experience of the brand (i.e. what you actually see, touch, smell or taste). The guiding principle by which the brand will always act. The touchstone.

Well, forget all that stuff. All you need to be clear about is your brand's positioning.

By the way we've included a very helpful glossary, The Lexicon of Brand, at the end of this book – courtesy of WHAM (an excellent brand consultancy who's clients include 3, Peroni and MTV), listing all the terms you hear in branding and marketing. So, if you just want to know what they mean, skip the rest of this chapter and flick through the Lexicon of Brand on page 185.

What is brand positioning?

Brand positioning is not where you put it on the shelf – nor if you move it from the bottom to the top shelf are you repositioning the brand.

---

[1] OK, we made this one up.

Brand positioning, put at its simplest, is: *what you want your brand to be famous for in the minds of your consumers or customers.* That's all.

You can position your positioning against your competitors' "positionings" by creating a 2 × 2 matrix. This ingenious device will help you see how close to your competitors you are – and where the gaps in the market are (depending on how saturated your market is). This is actually the best use of the 2 × 2 as opposed to the ubiquitous moving from bottom left to top right matrix scenario.

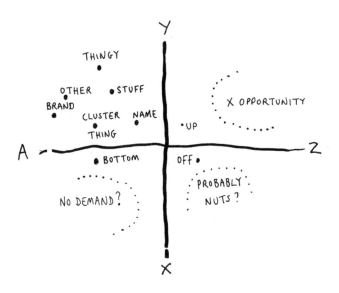

To define your positioning, you have to understand two things about your customers:

1 What is their defining characteristic?

2 What is their enduring need?

These are simple questions and the answers are simple. But the process of getting to the answer is very difficult.

A good example of this is the household-name washing powder who, after months of agonising, decided that the defining characteristic of its target consumer was "busy" and that their enduring need was "pleasure of deep cleaning first time".

This might sound simple but is, in fact, genius. Because it is clear and unequivocal. It is easy to understand how to position yourself against that need and thus what you need to be famous for.

And it fulfils two key criteria when thinking about how to describe your target audience.

1 It describes a characteristic about their attitude to life or the way they live their life, not a dull demographic description – they aren't 25–45-year-old mothers, they are "busy".

2 The "enduring need" is described as an emotional or psychological need, not a functional one – they don't need clothes cleaned, they want "pleasure". Think about it: if you are a busy person, you can't leave the house with a shirt or dress still carrying a stain, can you? What would that say about you?

Once you identify the defining characteristic and enduring need, the positioning falls into place.

Disney is famous for being magical. It appeals to the child in all of us.

Who do you think Nike is targeted at? Sports professionals? Sports jocks?

Nike target "athletes", brilliantly defined as "if you have a body, you're an athlete". In other words, it's an attitude of mind: if you want to be a winner in the game of life, then Nike's for you. That's why Nike famously is associated with "the attitude of winning".

Disney is famous for being magical. It appeals to the child in all of us.

The important thing to remember with brand positioning is that you don't need everyone always to use exactly the same words about you to be sure that you have achieved the positioning. Apple, for example, is famous for liberating the creative in the individual. Brand scientists, however, might talk about "man not being subservient to machines", or advertising agencies like TBWA and its Chairman Jean Marie-Dru might talk about the "disruption" that was caused or that the proposition was about "tools for creative minds". Lots of people including the (most important) customer will have their own versions of what Apple stands for. But they will overlap and cluster so as to play back the intended positioning. So if one person thinks it's "human" or another "creative" or another more technical person calls it "user friendly" – they are all, essentially, describing and *buying into* the same brand.

The other important thing to remember is that Apple delivered "creativity" with products such as the iMac, before it started evolving its communication look or identity.

How to write a brand positioning

Some companies like long positioning statements that include the product description, key benefit, reason to believe that benefit, the target audience, etc.

These are preferred particularly by traditional fast-moving consumer goods businesses. Here's an example.

> **Powerex** is the brand of detergent that cleans deep down due to its biological action because anxious people want the reassurance of fragrant clothes first time.

You can see how to join the dots.

> **Powerex** is the brand of *detergent* that *cleans deep down* due to its *biological action* because *anxious people* want the *reassurance of fragrant clothes first time.*
> **Brand name** is the *product category* that *product benefit* due to *reason to believe* because *target audience* want *enduring need.*

Others prefer to focus on the key phrase that determines what they want to be famous for; this is especially helpful when you have a single brand that spans over a number of product or service categories, such as Tesco's internal mantra "better, simpler, cheaper", which is translated into the strapline "every little helps".

You decide which works best for you. But remember your positioning must:

- tell people what you want to be famous for;
- respond directly to the enduring need of your target customer.

If you do that, you really don't need to worry about essences, DNA, philosophies and all that. Amusing though it might be to watch the marketing team tie themselves up in intellectual knots and consume vast research budgets to distil the essence of the brand down to one word. And fascinating though it might be to watch the PowerPoint presentation reveal that BA's one-word essence could be "favourite". It is of limited practical use. Or, put it this way, you will have learned nothing more than if you had just started off saying, "We want to be the airline everyone likes" and it would have cost you a lot less.

Right, that's positioning sorted.

Now there are just values and personality to deal with. But, you know what, we'll deal with them in the next two chapters.

The difference between product brands and corporate brands

People often ask, what is the difference between a product brand and a corporate brand? And the answer is simple: one is a brand that is used to sell a specific product and one is a brand that is used to sell a corporation. That's it.

Product brands tend to be associated with a limited range of offers, e.g. Persil brands detergents, and are always used to sell to consumers/customers. Corporate brands are often associated with a wide range of categories and are communicated sometimes only to employees or investors (e.g. Compass Group) but sometimes also to customers or consumers (e.g. Virgin) and sometimes somewhere in between, e.g. Unilever or Ford Motor Company and Ford Mondeo. And this leads us into the tricky, but now extremely important, area of brand architecture.

The importance of brand architecture (and what it means)

Brand architecture is the term used to refer to the way a business organises the various products and services it can offer under its brand or brands.

Put simply, there are three main approaches:

1 *Monolithic or single brand*, e.g. the BMW car brand. It uses only alpha-numeric indicators for its products because it wants people to focus on one brand only, i.e. BMW. (So although some of its cars, like the M3, may enjoy cult status, the personalities of the cars themselves are not made into a brand. Instead the models are described within an organised, predictable and clear system – which is very German of course.)

2 *Endorsed*, e.g. the Ford car or Nestlé food brands. They want you to buy more from their trusted sign, of course, but they sell so many different things (in Nestlé's case from chocolate bars to

coffee jars) or to different types of people (in Ford's case the Ka kid to the Mondeo man) that they need clearly defined and separately positioned sub-brands to target them.

3 *Freestanding brands*, e.g. Procter & Gamble or Compass Group where the business has such diverse activities, or even owns more than one brand in a market, and thus wants to keep itself invisible and let the individual brand build its own relationship with its specific consumer.

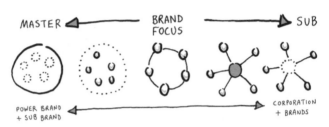

BASIC RANGE SHOWING BALANCE BETWEEN MASTER + SUB BRANDS.

But then it all starts to get confused because:

■ people use lots of different terms to describe these three basic approaches, e.g. range brand, house brand, master brand, simple branding, power branding;

■ people often confuse a true brand that has a distinct positioning and a clear promise of value with a product that has a bit of branding on it;

■ companies in innovation-heavy areas like telecoms or financial services (i.e. where they're always dreaming up new ways of selling you things) tend to get an idea and want to slap a name on it without thinking about whether it justifies being a brand or not;

- companies also tend to use variations of the three and don't just stick to one approach so BMW Group has a freestanding approach to its brand portfolio (Mini, Rolls Royce, BMW), each of those house brands uses either a monolithic or heavily endorsed approach and Mini uses BMW-branded spare parts as an ingredient. BMW is also very careful to keep reasonably apart its motorcycle and cars division.

Brand architecture is about making it easier for consumers to find what they want from you.

It also depends on how pedantic you want to be. We could bore you a lot more with the BMW example. The reality is modern brands are complex as, at another level, is the brand model of BMW. However, as long as the owner's focus matches what the majority of the customers think – then the brand model is working. So if BMW focuses on the BMW brand and most drivers think they drive a BMW as opposed to a 318ci then the model is working. They are buying into the monolithic over the product, sub or freestanding brand. That means they will be more likely to buy another model next time or recommend the brand to a friend.

You could argue that iPod is a freestanding brand because people buy into iPod, but actually they are buying into Apple. And, since iMac was the catalyst for all the "i" prefixes to iPod, iTunes, iLife, they now all support Apple as a monolithic brand.

It helps us to understand the brand model at this overall impression level and not at a micro level. Otherwise you can find yourself in meetings where the conversations go something like this: "Is it a range brand from the master brand or is it a sub-brand of the mother brand, or are we going to have to look at a partner brand that syncs with the house brand but is actually operating more like a freestanding brand but with a light endorsement from the corporate brand?"

Really, these conversations do happen. Think about that. The amount of client time and money that is wasted on such futile discussions. And still no one is any nearer to a clear and consistent answer. All we need to agree is that there are three main approaches and everyone can mix and match according to their specific corporate need. Think of the time we'd save that actually could be spent on doing something useful like, oh we don't know, improving the product, the advertising, the customer service, etc., etc.

Simple rules to follow in developing your brand architecture

Anyway, here are a few rules:

1 You can have as many products and services as you like but keep your brands down to a minimum.

2 Assume therefore that any new product or initiative can fit into your existing brand unless proven otherwise.

You can have as many products and services as you like but keep your brands down to a minimum.

3 You put your brand on what people think you are famous for or what you want to be famous for, we'll call this "the source of value", and don't put it on anything else. This is why BMW-branded spare parts in the Mini work. Mini's source of value is the exciting, cool, chic runaround car, not the brilliant engineering inside. BMW's source of value is in the brilliant engineering; it is the "ultimate driving machine".

4 You use simple descriptive naming or alpha-numerics to give customers information to help them find precisely what they want from your brand.

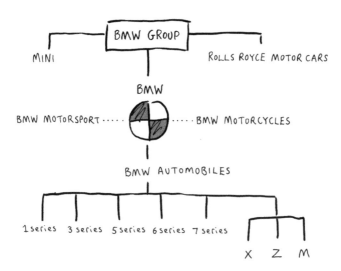

Positioning versus proposition

Another way to think of the difference in brand architecture terms between brands and product names is to think of the difference between positioning and proposition.

Positionings are expressed in the brand name – it's the source of value. Propositions are expressed in simple descriptors – it's the specific information that helps you get the particular product, service, offer you need. For example: Gap and M&S are both brands but they often offer several different propositions to their target audiences. You go to Gap, you want Menswear, or Winter Wear or clothes that are 'Stretch Tight' or 'Easy Fit'.

You see the difference? Easy Fit is not really a brand. It's a named proposition from the brand Gap.

How and when to create sub-brands

One of the questions that we frequently get asked by anyone from a CEO to a brand manager is, "How do I stop people from coming up with new names for their new product ideas all the time?"

Well, this is simple. First, if you're the CEO, then act like a CEO. You're the boss, remember. You let everyone know that no product or service will leave the door of your building with its own brand name or logo until it has been through the brand management team and that the brand management team reports directly to the CEO. And, if you are not the CEO, go and get the support of the CEO or the relevant Big Power. Remember, unless you have that ultimate authority behind you, you will struggle and, usually, fail.

Then you subject every new product or service idea to a brutally simple decision process comprising two things:

1 a "decision tree" about where to fit the product or service in your brand portfolio;

2 a "decision tree" about how exactly to name and identify it.

You need both these things.

It works something like this.

First, do we need to create a new brand or sub-brand?

1 Is this product or service something that fits what we want our brand to be famous for?

   If yes, go to question 2. If no, either abandon it or give it a different brand (go to naming and identity guidelines at the end of these questions).

2 Are we the only people responsible for delivering this to customers, i.e. is there any third party involved who could affect the perceived quality of the experience?

   If no, go to question 3. If yes, go to naming and identity guidelines at the end of these questions.

3 Is this (a) essentially the same product or service but in a new format, channel or a new audience but with the same needs (e.g. it's Ariel but in a tab form not a powder, it's Tesco but delivered to your door direct, it's Calvin Klein fragrance but for women not men, it's Gap but for kids)?

   Or (b) similar but with an ownable and unique feature or benefit or targeted at an audience with an additional need?

▶

If (a) go to question 4, if (b) create a sub-brand (go to naming and identity guidelines at the end of the questions).

4 Having got this far, is this so risky and are we so inexperienced in this category that we could really f*** up our logo?

If yes, create a sub-brand (go to naming and identity guidelines at the end of these questions). If no, give it the simplest product descriptor possible and launch it under our brand.

Naming and identity guidlines

Naming and identity guidelines are a bit trickier because you need the designers and naming craftsfolk to actually select the right one but, nevertheless, you should be able to get these guidelines down to four levels as follows:

1 Our brand + simple descriptor, e.g. Guinness Draft.

2 Our brand + sub-brand, e.g. Guinness Enigma.

3 Sub-brand + our brand, e.g. Kaliber from Guinness.

4 New brand, e.g. Harp (if you look on the small print round the back you'll see it's made by Arthur Guinness, though the Harp symbol is a subliminal reference too).

And, if you're working with a third party, then the naming and identity guidelines are still the same but the decision behind them is based on this element of risk:

1 No risk, e.g. Virgin Money (which uses RBS operations, not that consumers know that).

2 We need them to supply a bit of "magic" that we don't have, e.g. IBM with Intel Inside (where you're IBM).

3 We supply a bit of magic to them, e.g. IBM with Intel Inside (where you're Intel).

4 We can make money out of this but we don't want to risk our logo, e.g. Royal Bank of Scotland supplies Virgin Money.

Well, we've given this one away for free but you can make up your own – one that is right for your organisation. And it is vital that you do. In the end the way the architecture comes alive is specific for your brand.

Andy loves Playmobil – totally monolithic architecture – no product names – and the way you're guided around the brand is by age level and by the type of toy that you can see on the pack (cowboy, knights, spacemen, etc.). What it shows is that brand architecture is not about beardy strategy folk solving decision trees but intelligent branders understanding how to use their brand's specific assets to make life easier for them and consumers. Remember, beards can be cool, "chicks dig 'em", but decision trees are best left in the office, with a bit of grey water.

Jon loves cars; they're brilliant at organising information between source of value (brand) and specific information to help you make your choice and a great example of the rational and emotional appeal of a brand coming together.

The big players are masters of the balloon model of branding, i.e. playing off the quality brands (lifting the image of the portfolio like a balloon) versus the dead weight brands that drag down equity and trust.

The more complex the business, potentially the more complex things can get, but your choice of approach must be based on what is right for *you*, not what is the conventional practice of your category or competitors.

Consider the different, but equally effective, approaches of Tesco plc and The John Lewis Partnership.

John Lewis creates Waitrose as part of its partnership – branding it separately from the department store. Waitrose partners the Ocado brand of home delivery internet shopping – with a fresher, younger "early adopter" feel to its online experience. It also provides further disassociation from John Lewis and its more traditional, and maybe mature, customers. Waitrose also has WaitroseDeliver (online shopping). John Lewis also created Greenbee, which offers online purchase of concert tickets and selected products and is venturing into territories such as broadband. Ocado offers Greenbee services and so does the Waitrose site.

The John Lewis Partnership is pretty open with its association and cross-fertilisation of brands but keeps closer ties to its John Lewis and Waitrose brands and allows brands such as Ocado and Greenbee to be separate enough to have their own audience and so not compromise the John Lewis brand if they failed. John Lewis food hall stocks Waitrose products and Waitrose sells John Lewis furnishings and selected products. Its Waitrose stores do not sub-brand or feel the need to describe themselves by size. You can work out for yourself that a bigger store will have more products and a smaller store may be more selective. John Lewis maintains an upmarket brand portfolio by focusing on the idea of partnership. Each brand has a link, but very much its own brand identity. It puts quality or service at the top of its agenda.

Tesco, on the other hand, has built a brand on valuing value. Every venture is branded Tesco. Tesco home insurance, TescoCompare, Tesco motor insurance, Tesco petrol and so on. It all feeds back into the main brand. Tesco was also one of the first UK supermarkets to embrace and promote its own-label packaging, moving away from the trend of "me-too" packaging that copied the visual language of the market leaders. So the whole is greater than the sum of the parts. When it comes to its supermarkets, Tesco uses sub-brands such as Metro for smaller inner-city stores and Tesco Extra for bigger out-of-town stores.

This explicitly tells you that you can expect the same Tesco value but explains its propositions through the sub-brands. The pay-off for Metro is convenience but we do not expect as much variety or stock as a bigger supermarket. An out-of-town store like Extra will not be as convenient to get to, but the pay-off will be more choice and more products such as textiles, electrical goods and so on, under one roof.

Both businesses operate in similar markets and are leaders in what they do.

But their models are different. Tesco really spells out the propositions for its stores by creating names for them. The stores are almost sub-brands but weak ones that depend on the Tesco brand. Effectively, Tesco is a monolithic brand in the way it names and handles its UK portfolio. The John Lewis Partnership does not actively seek to "hide" the links between its various companies in any legal way, and it is organic in the way it has started to pull its brands closer together. But to consumers, it is essentially a freestanding brand architecture. The strategies of Tesco and John Lewis are different and pretty clear and consumers seem to understand them. Have you heard of any consumer writing to Tesco or John Lewis to complain about their brand architecture?

In the end brand architecture is about how you make it easiest for consumers to find what they want from you. Remember that "what they want" means the information you give them to make their specific choice; and "you" means your brand, the source of added value you bring to them.

Now, how to make all that strategy stuff visible to your customers or consumers? Well, it's over to those clever boys and girls with their colouring pens …

❝

Imagination is more important than knowledge.

Albert Einstein

APPLES, ORANGES, BLACKBERRYS AND OTHER FRUIT™

How to create a great brand identity

Perhaps the biggest culprit in the confusion of what branding really means is the logo designer.

Flick open the pages of the design press (they are populated by stories fed to them by advertising and design agencies of *all* shapes and sizes) and you will probably have a logo count higher than any nipple count in one of the less serious Sunday papers. Now, if the readers of those Sunday papers complained about the nipple count being too high you would think they were mad. And if the photographers that supplied the papers with the photos of breasts complained that they never bothered to show their sensitive or abstract portraits, then you would think them mad too.

Unfortunately, it's similar with graphic designers. Some designers are obsessed with the logo and clients are obsessed with the logo too. If the brand swear-box™ was introduced into design companies then you could ruin the industry if you made people pay 10 pence every time they used the word brand when they really meant logo. So, if the dudes paying for, and the dudes selling, "brand" are obsessed with logos, and the design industry's own press are subsequently fed logos, logos and more logos (including the occasional logotype, wordmarque, avatar, symbol, icon, etc., etc., etc.) *then* is it any wonder that the red tops, pink pages or six o'clock news latch on like a pit bull to the logo when a "brand" comes under fire.

The point is, the logo is not the whole brand identity, let alone the brand. It's easy to tut at the apparently philistine public who simply don't use enough unnecessary German words and who think that a million-squillion pounds have been blown on, say, the London Olympics logo (alone) and that their taxes are somehow responsible for every brand faux pas, from the BT logo, Consignia or PwC/Monday name change to the Kipling cake box that gets a fresh look and feel. But some of us in the MAD (Media, Advertising and Design) world have not helped by over-estimating the power of the logo alone. There are more important things to worry about. See the Implication Axis, which will explain why designers (or marketing, brand advertiser people) ought to calm down a bit.

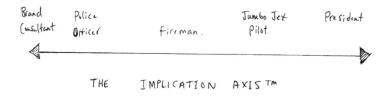

THE IMPLICATION AXIS ™

As proliferators, we must take account of what we do. The more we hide behind the logo for the lack of substance of a brand, the more the logo will become the burning flag of the anti-brandalists. Coke is it, not its logo – it's the Coke brand that is the dream. We all love the Apple logo, but it's the products, the stores, the service, the after sales that mean we pay a premium for the *brand*.

Of course, the logo is important as it is often the most visible part, the tip of that iceberg, the epitome, the thing on the football shirt, baseball cap, mouse mat, van livery, mobile phone, carrier bag, or, if you're really flash, laser or lenticular and therefore it is one of the most "touchable" and sometimes aspirational or desirable parts of the brand. It's eventually what goes on products, etc. – your business card. Our personal favourite was a guy abroad trying to sell a logo asking the-owner of a multi-national if he'd "like it on his tie", which is a nice benchmark. Everyone will have a view on it, from the chairman and the chairman's wife to Doris in accounts, etc. We've never understood this because, actually, it's not easy. Even great designers probably can't claim more than a couple, if even one, of the top 100 brands, logos or identities.

What is brand identity?

Brand identity means the various visual and verbal signs that distinguish and are owned by your brand and which are used to identify, communicate and protect your brand in the marketplace.

Brand identities can consist of:

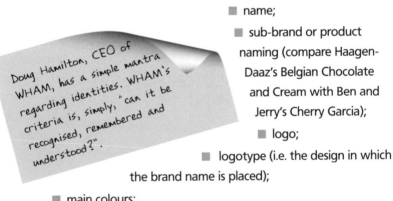

Doug Hamilton, CEO of WHAM, has a simple mantra regarding identities. WHAM's criteria is, simply, "can it be recognised, remembered and understood?".

- name;
- sub-brand or product naming (compare Haagen-Daaz's Belgian Chocolate and Cream with Ben and Jerry's Cherry Garcia);
- logo;
- logotype (i.e. the design in which the brand name is placed);
- main colours;
- secondary colour palettes;
- secondary graphic device (e.g. the Coke ribbon);
- image style (photography, illustration, etc.);

- sonics (e.g. jingles, ringtones);
- layouts for print (brochures, poster ads, etc.);
- tone of voice (vocabulary and style).

And they have to be managed across everything from a business card to a website.

The brand strategy informs and translates into the identity, or maybe it is better to say that the brand strategy is transformed into the identity by the power of a creative idea.

So this chapter isn't about how to design the ultimate logo, it is about making you see you need to consider all the other relevant components that you will need to make up your identity.

Doug Hamilton, CEO of WHAM, has advised clients such as Orange and First Direct on their branding and has a simple mantra regarding identities. WHAM's criteria is, simply, "can it be recognised, remembered and understood?".

Expressing values and personality

What brand identity does best is express your brand's personality and communicate its values. This may be done literally (or obviously) or maybe emotionally (or by suggestion). This is why we get no-nonsense brands like Microsoft and more emotional brands like Orange. This bit will be subject to taste and design, how the client thinks and how the agency thinks. The strategy of the brand ought to add up to the expression of the brand (its identity), in the same way that we judge a person by how they act and what they actually do. So too with brands.

You choose to associate yourself or not with people that hold similar values or characteristics. Maybe you are attracted to younger people with a relevant ambition (vision) or that are on a positive journey (mission). And so it goes on.

A haircut is a good analogy. Logos are to brands as haircuts are to people. Not many of us have the guts to ask the hairdresser to cut our hair to suit our face.

Brand identity makes the strategy bit human. And you wouldn't suggest a person had no values or a rubbish personality, so of course you wouldn't suggest that of your brand either. No, you want a person who behaves in the way you like with the right experience, knowledge and credibility to perform certain tasks whether that be a soldier, brain surgeon, cab driver (bigger hippocampus) or bus driver. So too, you would make sure some brands delivered the right items or behaved appropriately and had relevance or credibility in their sectors and markets.

A haircut is a good analogy. Logos are to brands as haircuts are to people. Not many of us have the guts to ask the hairdresser to cut our hair to suit our face. And the same is true with brands and logos. We want the Brad Pitt haircut – when what we really want is to be Brad Pitt. Haircut ain't gonna do it.

And people kinda get this too. Try shaving your head or radically cutting your hair and see how many people think you're having a mid-something crisis.

On the other hand, flares will eventually come back in, so keep rockin' the same look for long enough and you'll eventually be as authentically cool as you were once genuinely unfashionable. Your choice. The point is that image shouldn't be separated from behaviour. If it's at odds – you'll get misunderstood and no one will like you.

How do you "own" a brand identity in the market?

Apart from through legal protection, which we cover in Chapter 8, brands don't own colour, type, people or lines. Get real – you can trademark things, but there's no point "owning" an identity unless it's by law. Better to occupy a position and seek to make your identity clear and consistent so it is always associated with you. There are three things you need to do to get that association with your brand identity in people's minds.

1 Be different – ensure that the way you look and what you say is unique, or at least clearly differentiated from any competitor in your market. You might even go so far as to challenge some of the "visual" rules in a marketplace. For example, in the UK crisps market, for years, blue was the colour everyone used for salt and vinegar flavoured crisps and green for cheese and onion. Then Walkers crisps decided that they would reverse that colour coding for their own brand. Far from confusing consumers, it helped Walkers to stand out. Although it's worth remembering that difference is a supporting factor to what you do and should not to be relied on for the sake of it. A similar strategy adopted by Pepsi to "own blue" versus the conventions of the red colour packaging of the cola market hasn't changed the market in quite the same way.

2 Be consistent – when you have developed your brand identity, stick to it, use it wherever you can and should and don't let anyone in your organisation mess around with it. Consumers need to find you and recognise you.

3 Be relevant. Don't slap your logo everywhere like a dog marking out its territory. Don't swamp the world with your colour, like you were polluting the environment. And don't try too hard to be clever with your branding. It can really annoy people – like the tampon story we'll tell you about in a little while.

Before we go into the rest of the rules of brand identity there is one law that you must obey…

LAW 1 – GET YOURSELF A GOOD NAME

We could have written a chapter about brand naming alone. In fact there are whole chapters in other brand books about this. In fact there are even whole books on the subject.

We didn't want to go on and on about brand naming but we did want you to realise that this is *very important*. Because if you don't have a brand name, you don't have a brand. So we've put this section in a box, so you know it's important. The first thing to say is that everything has been done or at least registered so don't worry about trying to get the dot.com – you can find a way around that later. Registering your name and identity as a trademark is the key factor.

There are naming agencies that specialise in this because it is harder than it looks. If you have ever tried to name a child, you'll know what we mean. You like one name, your partner likes another. Oh and then when you find a name you both like, you can't have it because Cousin Avril has just called her fifth child that name and, anyway, naming the kid after a character in *Dungeons and Dragons* doesn't seem as cool as it once was, etc., etc. Well, naming a brand is harder and more expensive.

The truth is that naming can happen at any stage of the brand creation process. Some people start off with a name and are desperate for a brand they can use it on (like a friend of ours who wants to brand something Adverb, he just doesn't know what). Sometimes it's done at the very last moment when the product is about to hit the market (like the story of the cars which had been built in the factory and were just waiting for someone to call them Mini Metro before they could be launched). But it's best if naming is done after the strategy and at the early stages of the identity.

But, whenever you do it, there are four things *only* that *you must* do when selecting a brand name:

1 Decide whether you want your name to describe what you do or express a personality (e.g. France Telecom or Orange) – it can't do both equally.

2 Decide whether you want the "tone" of your name to be serious or playful (e.g. IBM or Apple) – it can't be both.

3 Check whether your name is culturally offensive or risible overseas – someone in Norway really thought Nora Knackers was a good name for a crisp bread.

4 Have a trademark lawyer tell you how to protect it!

Naming is a specific issue we had to mention separately but there are other important rules we want you to think about in creating a great brand identity.

Rules to follow to create a great brand identity

Simple – give us a million-billion-skillion pounds. Easy.

Or just as simple, but harder, follow the rules listed below.

By the way we've gathered all the rules we set out in each chapter of this book into one easy-to-find list at the end of the book. So, if you're bored by all this reading you can just skip to those rules on page 172.

Rule 1 – Get a simple, short, creative idea

There are lots of legends in the branding business, many of which harp back to the 1980s – some of them told by people who weren't even there. We were still at school in the early 1980s, when brand really was image and when white Testarossas and shirts with different collars were cool. Our favourite tales include ad agencies parking cars in lifts or keeping British Rail waiting in reception for 45 minutes (you'll also hear 2 hours/day/week – depending on the teller) to point out how their customers apparently were treated. But what they were very good at in the 1980s was having a great creative idea that said something truthful and relevant in a surprising way. Like how Ridley Scott et al. pitched to get funding for the film *Alien*, by describing it as "Jaws in space". Easy to get, eh? From the design side of things a simple creative idea will make a holistic approach much easier. If you can understand the whole from the sensibility of the smaller components then the whole really is greater than the sum of the parts.

The creative idea needs to be built on and relate to the brand strategy. It needs to avoid the generic aspects that may come out of the strategy.

The best creative start points will be the simplest, shortest descriptions.

Rule 1 really is to make sure there is a strong central idea to the brand.

If not, you will have to make one up – and possibly this will become a process of post-rationalising the creative work based on fashion or taste.

Rule 2 – Start thinking about the "feeling" of the brand early on

You may find your first ideas are the best, but you'll probably not crack it all first off, and you'll more than likely end up trialling/developing various concepts simultaneously. Your various ideas should cluster – you'll start to find that there's a pliable, mouldable feeling that connects the various ideas. You should be able to have a look and layout using a slave name – one that you will recognise if you change the name or colour. In the early stages of the development, mood boards are actually of use. You can afford to be freer and looser with the look and feel. By grabbing images of existing brands in other sectors, or photography, typefaces, tonal communication, you should also be able to gather a look and feel that is consistent or starts to paint the picture you want your brand to live in.

Rule 3 – Learn to be objective

Try not to fall in love with (normally your own) ideas too quickly, you need to remain clear on what will be best for the brand and most understood by the users or customers. Don't get into a beauty parade too early, by which we mean don't start judging immediately the idea that is presented to you on face value. Don't get wedded to one particular name, colour, typeface, etc. too early. Chances are the name you want won't be available anyway. Try and stay objective, sleep on it.

If you think you've got a brilliant original identity, dream on – it's all been done before. We guarantee that whatever you've come up with you'll see a similar, if not identical, idea, colour, concept or line used in an ad for coffee, mobiles, tampons – you name it. And if there's not one now – there's always some nerd who will point out how they thought of it before or that there was one like that in green in 1963, when everything was seen in black and white anyway.

Rule 4 – Follow what you believe in and don't worry about literal meaning

Developing brand identity is like art. Traditional art had to be understood. The search for the photographic before anyone even knew what photography meant. Realism, truth. So art's job was to record. Similarly, early branding's role was to let people know what the product was or did. BMW's logo is based on a propellor because, when it started as a company, that's what it made, long before it made cars. Modern art instills the same "my three-year-old could have done better" response in that man in the street who is about to pick up the paper again and phone in about the latest logo – faster than you can say, "Blow me! What the bleeding hell next? That looks like a dead shark in formaldehyde being b******d by Homer Simpson – how many millions of taxpayers' money have they spent now? This is an outrage!!!"

The difference being it's par for the course to innovate, disrupt or self-indulge in the undignified or private joke of the art world. It's personal expression. Rarity and narrative are drivers in collectability. But Picasso wasn't looking to create evolutions of the Kipling cake box for the masses. He was tearing down boundaries. "Ooh, that looks like a Rothko," is a polite way of saying simultaneously I don't know much about modern art and you can't paint. But of course Rothko could paint. You can feel the remorse, the pain in his paintings. They won't always brighten up the room. Picasso could draw. He was a master craftsman. He didn't just go straight into cubism. It was a natural progression in his interrogation of the world around him. A picture could paint a thousand words – but an abstract form could ensnare the soul. So it is now with branding. It is less about what the brand owner wants to tell you and more about what he wants to allow you to feel.

Michaelangelo didn't just "paint the ceiling", he also designed the whole damn joint.

So consider how the mood, tone and visual style makes you feel. What does it remind you of? What sector will people think it fits in? What is the age group it is aimed at? Is it upmarket or value-conscious? What street does it belong on? Start to embrace the visceral qualities of what you are developing.

Rule 5 – Be inspired by other brands but don't copy

Let's keep the art analogy going. Michaelangelo didn't just "paint the ceiling", he also designed the whole damn joint. Similarly Apple's success has very little to do with its logo. Sorry, but true. Even if you like the logo, you really love what it stands for – what the brand does. So if you try and paint like Rothko cos red is your favourite colour, or you fancy a bit of Guernica in your bathroom, "How hard can it be?" – if you borrow the look without walking the path – it'll be rubbish. Similarly, if you borrow the clothes from another brand, without doing the delivery bit – the results will be sh*t. Remember, copycats don't get to lick the cream.

Rule 6 – Understand the areas in which your identity needs to operate

Understand what your business's competition is and what the market looks like.

Be real about where your brand *will really be seen* – either by the market or where you can afford, or are able, to place it. So – if you're a dot.com or a butcher – where's your audience?

Don't be so quick to let the design of the advert take over. What about the other ways that people will touch the brand? It's what the marketing dudes nowadays call "touchpoints". If your business is built by word of mouth then your identity has to facilitate that. If you are a shop then you've already got a great promotional space called your shop window and mobile advertising placards called shopping bags. Think about the UK haulier Eddie Stobart's trucks and vans. They're adverts on wheels. And they've become a range of toys too.

Rule 7 – Don't worry about "will it fax?"

You'll see then how you need to produce your identity, online or print? Does it need to work on TV or fax? As a form or an unsexy invoice?

Don't keep repeating the branding everywhere, writing "Push me please, oh go on," in an annoying on-message way on every door in your HQ that will just p**s everyone off. Instead, understand that if, for example, you're mainly online, you can have as much colour as you want – or there will be more time for it to move, behave like an animation, etc., etc.

Here's a funny story. A well-known sanitary towel brand had "Have a Happy Period" written on the inside. Great tone of voice. Really on-brand, right? However. It drove one woman so mad that she wrote a letter to the brand manager. Few people seem sure if the original letter was authentic, but it was emailed all round the world and appeared on many websites, because other people shared her irritation. As she said in the letter:

Are you f***ing kidding me? What I mean is, does any part of your tiny middle-manager brain really think happiness – actual smiling, laughing happiness, is possible during a menstrual period?

… there will never be anything 'happy' about a day in which you have to jack yourself up on Motrin and Kahlua and lock yourself in your house just so you don't march down to the local Kmart armed with a hunting rifle and a sketchy plan to end your life in a blaze of glory.

… If you just have to slap a moronic message on a maxi pad, wouldn't it make more sense to say something that's actually pertinent, like 'Put down the Hammer' or 'Vehicular Manslaughter is Wrong', or are you just picking on us? Sir, please inform your Accounting Department that, effective immediately, there will be an $8 drop in monthly profits, for I have chosen to take my maxi-pad business elsewhere …

Rule 8 – Ask yourself how long this identity should last

How long is the product's shelf life?

How often do people in that sector rebrand?

How much will it cost you to rebrand?

Can you update without looking like another business?

Are you a monolithic business or do you need to constantly surprise through sub-branding? If the latter, will these look like or need to look like the parent, etc? (See Chapter 4.)

Rule 9 – Give people the tools to join in with, not just implement, the brand

There's a big difference between coherency and consistency. What will work best for *your brand* not just you. Will you be open and expansive – or call the brand police if people don't use a full stop in the right. place

Rule 10 – Be wary of visual clichés

Here are the top 10 most used visual ideas in branding. Make sure the designers you use are not just throwing one of these at you.

1   The aperture or gateway – basically an excuse to stick stuff in the 'O' or any part or shape of your name.

2   The simple geometric shape.

3   The "person-shaped figure". This is usually sold with the explanation that "people engage with people more than type"

(which means your name is sh*t and so let's make it into a friendly face or little man – a bit like seeing dragons in cloud formations).

4 Lower case.

5 The colon or asterisk.

6 The globe.

7 The non-logo – an excuse to use a new typeface bought for another client that didn't use it.

8 The unique colour route (almost always purple).

9 The ripped-off logo not used any more from *Los Logos* book or from 10 years ago.

10 Using/emphasising a misspelling, use of a z or an x – or flipping a letter backwards or upside down.

We've sketched a few of them for you so you can spot them in future. In fact that could be a good game to play on a long car journey as you pass by the proliferations of logos that surround us. Can you spot the aperture? Did you see the lower case? Umm … OK maybe not such a fun game for the kids, best to stay listening to the radio.

FILL THIS
WITH STUFF...
THE APERTURE™

friendly™

LOWERCASE

GLOBE
or
PLANET

THE
INFINITY
THINGY™

Rule 11 – Never launch a logo and pretend it's a brand

Remember the BA tailfins? On the one hand a very forward-thinking approach to identity. But it was quickly misunderstood and a bit of a flop. Arguably the BA stuff was a great idea but in the wrong place. With hindsight, it was wrong in 1997 to remove the Union Jack from the tailfins. That wasn't seen so much as updating a logo but perceived by the tabloid and *Telegraph* newspaper readers as equivalent to "burning the flag". The Union Jack had been replaced by international, or ethinic, art. Perhaps the global identities should have lived on the menus and the tickets, but maybe not the tailfin. But design aside, it was the reveal that was the problem. No momentum, no joined-up story about how the brand (i.e. the airline) was going to make the idea of a global citizen a reality. So what else did we expect Mrs Thatcher (a true-blue-come-on-England-remember-the-Falklands-I-can-drive-a-tank woman) to do? Out came the handkerchief and, fairly soon, off came the ethnic art tailfin designs.

And 10 or so years on, it was a similar story with the London Olympics logo. A bad reveal. Here's our new brand, I mean logo, I mean brand. But the logo ain't the brand. Don't reveal a logo then say that's the brand. The brand of the Olympics is sorted. It has been since 19whatnot. World peace, winning, taking part, etc. – the rings (the Olympic logo) stand for the universal values understood by what the Olympics is – which is awesome. Perhaps they should have only talked about the brilliance of the Olympics coming to London, the celebration, and majored on Zaha Hadid talking about the amazing new structures she's designed for the village; if there'd been more focus on the values. What about winning, Britain, the hopes and dreams of a new generation, etc., etc., etc? Instead we just saw loads of pictures of Seb Coe standing by the logo. Perhaps, like the tailfins, too futuristic an idea? Or a reveal that with hindsight put too much emphasis on the logo instead of the brand?

What the Olympics and BA shared was the power of a brand (not a logo) that the public felt they somehow had a part in – they are both sort of national institutions. Sure, everyone was talking about the logos when they were launched, there were lots of column inches in the press, but if that was the objective you might as well have just got Kylie Minogue to undress under the words "London 2012". So the lesson is: reveal a brand for people to live up to, not a logo you have to justify. And don't think that the public are wrong – they're not.

Reveal a brand for people to live up to, not a logo you have to justify.

Rule 12 – Let everyone else catch up and then evolve and keep evolving

All you can really do with your identity is make people remember you and make it easy for them to find you. When you do it well, others in your market will want to copy you, to ape your success. If you are perceived to own the colour Orange, they'll try and own the colour red, etc. Let them. The thing is there's more to brands than "owning colour". It's not actually a reason to put you off using a colour in your marketing or communications, is it? In any case you can't do much about it. And anyway, they have only just caught up to the first level of consistent brand image. If you do the simple, hard, maybe boring, but actually more satisfying, bit of working out what your customers need and want – and how you can meet them – then you can build a really differentiated brand. Then you can develop your identity to reinforce the experience people have of you. Then you will have reached brand karma. Buddha is as Buddha does. Brand is as brand does. And that's the next chapter.

> **Don't p*** in my pocket and tell me it's raining.**
>
> Dragan, *Layer Cake*

IT'S THE EXPERIENCE, STUPID!

*6

Here's another game you can play at home. Shut your eyes. Think of your favourite brand. Think of all the reasons you like it. Would you recommend it to someone else? To a friend? If so, why?

Now, open your eyes (oh, of course you can't cos you can't read this, cos your eyes are closed).

Well, anyway, when you thought of all the reasons you would recommend that brand to someone else, were any of those reasons: "You'll love the advertising"? If you answered yes, then you work in advertising or you used to work in advertising or want to work in advertising. Any other sane person would say no.

This is important. The future battleground of customer loyalty and customer advocacy (i.e. when one customer tells another customer that they "really, simply must buy this brand. No, I mean it, you'll love it, it's fantastic") is the customer experience. Not the _promise_ of value (which advertising tends to focus on) but the _actual_ value in the experience of buying and consuming the brand. Authenticity. That's the big word to get your teeth into. Be real.

As a BA marketing chief once put it: "One bad telesales experience can undo thousands of dollars of advertising."

Oh dear. So after you've sweated over your strategy, and pulled your hair and eyes out over choosing a name and logo, you now have to do the really hard bit and deliver your promise to your customers.

That means having products that are a joy to possess, or services that delight people; it means having people who work for you who impress the customer because they go the extra mile, having environments that create the right ambience and, when someone complains, going into overdrive to recover them.

Over the last dozen years or so, a trend has grown up measuring the satisfaction of a customer and how likely they are to buy more from you. It's now called "net promoter score" (NPS) but it used to be called customer delight. It says that on a 0–10-point scale of customer satisfaction, it is only if you are scoring 9/10 that you have a loyal customer. Every other customer is ripe for turning. And when they are scoring you that highly, they become advocates (or promoters, as Fred Reichheld, the inventor of the index, calls them) for your brand. The NPS (i.e. when you take the 0–6 ratings from the 9 and 10 ratings) is an index of what proportion of your business will come from word of mouth. Reichheld reckons that this is the "only number you need to grow" to be successful. Now, we should point out that a number of research companies think that the NPS score is bullsh*t and that it is dangerous to rely on just one number. They would say that, though, wouldn't they – it's like turkeys voting for Christmas.

Real-life anecdote No. 2

Seemingly everyone likes a moan about the foreign call centres and bad service, but Jon actually had a refreshingly brilliant experience recently with Dyson. He phoned the number on the vacuum when the appliance had stopped working properly in the middle of a Bank Holiday weekend. The guy that answered the phone promptly talked him through how to take it apart simply and reset it. Now, normally Jon would not have much faith in phoning such numbers, let alone on a Bank Holiday weekend – but what a brilliant experience. Reason to buy another one, or recommend the brand.

In fact, the anecdote about BMW used industry-wide quotes that more owners who experience the car going wrong are statistically more likely to buy another BMW, because of the great service they receive, than those who never encounter problems. The smart money these days is with brands that see the value in delighting their customers with service, before, during and after the sale.

Real-life anecdote No. 3

We heard a great Carphone Warehouse story the other day from a friend. She was trying to buy a *digital photo* frame as a Christmas present and had ordered it from Carphone Warehouse. On Christmas Eve it hadn't arrived and, when she went round to the store to see the manager, he said he was closing up for the day and could not help. She was distraught. Understandably. She had to race to WH Smith to buy one quickly. So she sent a stroppy email off to Carphone Warehouse and, lo and behold, someone called her up as soon as they got it. Listened to her rant. Empathised.

Apologised. And then, not only refunded her the money she had paid to WH Smith for a different digital photo frame but doubled the price. Was she happy now? You bet. Would she buy another digital photo frame from Carphone Warehouse? No. But she'd buy something else and she's told as many people as she can about that story and she usually ends with, "Wasn't that great of them?" And all the people she's told feel that Carphone Warehouse is a safe place to do their shopping.

And now we've told you that story (the hundreds of thousands of you who are buying this book). And now, admit it, you, even grudgingly, think a little better of Carphone Warehouse, don't you? Well, we bet some of you do.

The point of the net promoter score is that, if a customer is "promoting" your brand, then his or her recommendation is likely to be believed and genuinely influence the intention to buy your brand. And traditional and even non-traditional advertising cannot match the pure power of word-of-mouth recommendation. Never has been able to. No matter how many cars you've packed in a lift in your much talked about advert.

A recent study in the telco market showed that simply adding an extra one point on to your net promoter score would result in an extra £7.5 million revenue.

But, in order to earn a high net promoter score, you have to do one very brave thing.

You have to deliver the promise you make to the person to whom that promise is most valuable.

You have to deliver the promise you make to the person to whom that promise is *most valuable.*

Please note the phrase "the person to whom that promise is most valuable"– not everyone, not other people's customers, not necessarily all the people who have bought your brand. Only the people to whom your specific brand promise is most valuable.

This is called being customer-focused. It's different from being customer-driven. Customer-driven means customers tell us what to do. Customer-focused means we know what will delight our target customers and we focus on that.

Delivering a great customer experience takes six steps, which we will outline below – and not one of them involves f***ing with the logo.

Before we go on, though, a word of acknowledgement. The following six steps are courtesy of the company Smith and Co. Shaun Smith has advised more companies on how to develop outstanding customer experiences than probably anyone else and he has written the definitive book on the subject, *Managing the Customer Experience*. We rate it and it's included in the appendix. And we've kind of distilled it – in our own words – and some of Shaun's other thinkings for you here.

Step 1 Ask yourself the following: who are your target customers and what do they most value? What is their current experience like?

A customer's experience is defined as every time they encounter anything that carries your brand – from the time they see your ad to the time they call your number, speak to your staff, flick through your catalogue or webpage, shop at your store or buy online or meet your team, who are pitching or tendering for their money, to the time they are actually using your product to when they throw it away, pass it on or come back and buy more. Everything.

Smith says think about it like an ECG monitor. During their whole experience of you, when does their heart rate soar with joy or plunge with despair or bump along with little annoyances or just flatline cos they're bored to death?

To understand what your target customers most value, you need to actively watch, listen and talk to your customers as they are actually experiencing your brand in real life. Some companies put cameras in fridges to watch people as they use their ketchup, some walk round shops with people watching how they buy, some go and live with families for a week. Harley Davidson executives go out for rides with their customers. Richard Branson travels on his planes and trains, talking to his customers and employees, busily scribbling notes.

It doesn't matter how you get this information, what matters is that you focus on what it is that people are actually experiencing and what are the "peak moments" – peak moments are those moments when a customer's emotional response (good or bad) is at its highest *and* aligned with the brand values and promise. For example, the peak moment of pleasure when you travel with Virgin Airlines is probably when you get into their Clubhouse because their values include innovation and fun. Whereas the peak moment of pain with BA is when they lose your bag because BA is supposed to be about quality service – OK, we know they say it's not their fault and it's the airport's fault, but do you really care who lost it? No, you paid BA for the ticket not BAA, so that's whom you'll blame, probably.

by delivering on your promises, you establish your positioning in people's minds.

Step 2 What promises can our brand make that would distinguish us credibly and delight our customers during the experience?

A brand promise is the guarantees of service or product experience that you make to customers. "Never knowingly undersold" might be a tagline for John Lewis but it's also a promise. "Fresh ingredients", that's another. "Only sandwiches made on the day are sold in the store", that's another. "0–60 in 60 seconds" is another. They are not the brand positioning but by delivering on your promises, you establish your positioning in people's minds.

It's not good enough to just improve things. You have to have a point of view on how to improve things that fits with your brand positioning. It has to be something you want to be famous for. And it should be at a "peak" moment.

That means you have to look at any specific promise you make through the filter of your desired brand positioning, your values and personality.

Let's go back to the airline example. Virgin realised that, when a customer bought a plane ticket, the journey started when they left home. So there was an opportunity to differentiate. How did they do it? They didn't send a taxi round, they sent a branded limo to pick people up. In fact, if it was rush-hour traffic, they sent a branded limo-bike round. Sounds fun? Well, fun is one of Virgin's core values. Of course, the target customer in this case was the Upper Class customer who could afford (or whose company could afford) to pay for what it valued. Virgin Upper Class promises to get you from kerb-side, when your limo drops you off, into the Clubhouse within 10 minutes. They have eliminated most of the pain and bullsh*t that most of us have to endure at check-in and security.

Step 3 What do we need to do to our processes, people and products to deliver these promises?

This is where you get a group of people from within the business who are responsible for delivery, e.g. the operations people, the R&D people, the HR people, whoever it is in your organisation.

In a telco, for example, the people to bring together would be R&D, customer service, the HR and business operations people. In a bank it would be the product marketeers, the heads of lines of business (retail banking, corporate banking, private banking), IT, HR people. In an airline – the engineers, the cabin crew, the groundstaff, the product marketeers, the heads of regions, HR people. In an FMCG brand it would be R&D, marketing, heads of markets, HR. Big N.B.: it's always the HR and marketing people.

Basically, if you work through the touchline it's easy to see who you need to involve in creating the solutions.

Tell them what the promise is and give them a time frame in which they have to come up with the solution and what the budgets are and let them go away and work it out.

Step 4 Align your organisation with the promise.

Once the new product or service initiative is ready, make sure everyone in the company knows about it. Train those who need to know about it most before anyone else. Then let everyone else in the business know about it before it goes live. Align your processes and technology with your people so you can deliver the promise.

Remember the disastrous opening of Terminal 5 at Heathrow? What went wrong? One very simple thing: BAA and BA had not got their act together on the amount of time airline staff would need to be properly trained on, and know how to use, all the baggaging equipment. That's what happens when you don't align your technology and process with your people.

Real-life anecdote No. 5

The marketing team of a direct insurance business came up with a neat idea: offering discounts on holidays to people who bought holiday insurance with them. The adverts appeared. Then the call centres started getting the calls, which went like this:

Call centre: Good morning, how can I help you?

Customer: I'd like to book the holiday insurance deal please.

CC: Which deal would that be?

Customer: The one in the adverts.

CC: Which adverts?

Customer: The one I'm looking at offering me 10 per cent off a holiday if I book insurance with you.

CC: Oh ... hold on a moment ... (places hand over phone and asks supervisor). You heard anything about the holiday insurance deal?

Supervisor: Which deal would that be?

CC: The one in the advert.

Supervisor: Which advert?

Etc., etc.

Yes, the marketing team had not ensured that the call centres had been briefed properly for the floods of calls about the holiday deals. This need never happen again. Organisations like Cincom are bringing out new versions of call centre software like Synchrony that provide agents with all the tools, information and help they need to deliver the experience. As long as the marketing department tells them what to expect.

We think Diageo does the internal communication and alignment well. They *love* their brands. They really do. But then, since their brands are whiskies, gins, vodkas, etc. it's easy to be in love with them. They have teams of people who are sent on training courses in obscure Scottish castles near wonderfully ancient distilleries to learn about any new brand or new promotion. And nothing, but nothing, goes out the door until the trade, the production, the marketing are all ready and in place.

Step 5 Communicate externally.

Now you can go live with the viral campaigns, Web banners, cinema ads, street marketing or wall-to-wall TV ad coverage. Unleash the dogs of awe!

Sadly, we fear most people go from steps 1 to 5 without pausing on 2, 3 and 4.

Step 6 Measure it!

Is it working? Answering that means first being clear about what you wanted it to do.

Raise sales? Build profits? Increase awareness? Raise customer delight? Improve net promoter score? You choose. But whatever you choose, make sure you measure it.

If you want to find out more, go to www.shaunsmithco.com.

There, that's easy, isn't it?

Now then, about that measurement … that involves research, doesn't it? Which leads us on to our next chapter.

Research is always incomplete.

Mark Pattison

TOO MANY OPINIONS AND NOT ENOUGH CHEESE SANDWICHES

A bit about research

*7

OK, we'd better 'fess up here. We are not exactly uncritical fans of research. Now don't get us wrong, many of our friends are researchers, some of them are even market researchers. And it's not that we think research is unimportant. It is important. It's just that – and our researcher friends agree with us on this – research can get used so badly and everyone panics when they're told "We haven't researched this yet" and the research that is done is sometimes so poorly interpreted or misused to justify covering the corporate ass and ... and ... well, you know.

Here's what Benj Fearn, former UK marketing director of Nike told us:

> The thing that struck me about Nike was the way they used consumer insight – they didn't in any traditional sense. They were primary interested in brand insight. Understanding what was going on in consumers' minds – as well as in popular culture – was important to set the context in which you were operating, but nowhere near as important as having insights into what your brand could do to enrich that culture and influence consumer behaviour.

In other words, a lot more intuitive thinking was done about how to build and market the brand than slavish colour-by-numbers research. In fact, in Nike, the bulk of research budgets are spent on testing and improving the quality of the product performance or consumer experience, which is great, because that's what consumers really want.

Worse still, a lot of research is done just for the sake of doing it, with little thought being given to how it is to be used.

Insight UK, a company that knows of such things, estimated that 50 per cent of all research conducted in the UK was wasted.

In the book *See, Feel, Think, Do* there is this lovely story:

> One company spent close to US$1 million trying to understand what its customers valued. In all, 200 employees in 17 different departments were involved in 105 separate customer research activities. This sounds impressive, but unfortunately there were two major problems. First, the data collection effort was uncoordinated. Some customers were being contacted almost four times a month, and, not surprisingly, they often complained of being asked similar questions by different people for different purposes. The second problem was that the data collected in the company's US$1 million effort was not being used to improve much of anything. It just lay there. Only 43 per cent of the people who had collected the data reported it to anyone but themselves. Only 39 per cent said any action was taken as a result. Only 27 per cent of the information taken

from external customers was reported as "acted upon". It was as if most of the data so assiduously gathered had disappeared into a black hole.[1]

Understanding how to use and not to use research is vital in brand building. And especially important when it comes to the creative side of things. OK, here's where the management consultants and strategy folk roll their eyes and think, "If I hear another second-rate creative tell me his rubbishy idea can never be understood by a focus group so just trust your multi-million-dollar budget to my ego and launch, I'll scream". And they have a point. It's very easy to be cavalier about research when it's not your budget, not your brand. But the fact remains that well-researched products and ad campaigns fail and others launched on a wing and a prayer succeed.

Here are two examples:

1 innocent smoothies spent £500 on market researching their product. That was the cost of the stall they set up at a UK music festival, the fruit they used to make smoothies there and the two plastic bins marked yes and no into which they asked customers to throw their empties in response to the question: "Should we give up our day jobs and make smoothies for a living?"

They've got over £5 million turnover now.

2 BA spent [I don't want to tell you how much] on researching the global acceptability of its funky tailfins. And one ex-prime minister's handkerchief helped to have them all sprayed back to the Union Jack.

[1] *See, Feel, Think, Do*: Milligan and Smith (2007)

The point is that research only gets you so far, the rest is fate and faith. Actually, while we're on a roll, here's what people who have been involved in building some of the great brands we know and admire today say about research:

"Focus groups are a form of marketing séance – where gullible marketing folk believe they will be able to commune with the great unknown that is the consumer's mind."

"A rear view mirror – tells you what they thought six weeks ago, sometimes six months ago, not what they'll be thinking in six months' time."

"The only research I trust is the one I do when I go out into the shops and see what is actually happening and talk to customers and staff about what they see and feel."

"You need market research like you need car insurance – it's a necessary pain – but it's of less use than car insurance cos if something goes wrong you can't claim back from the research company."

"Focus groups are a form of marketing séance – where gullible marketing folk believe they will be able to commune with the great unknown that is the consumer's mind."

OK, so you have our (and many others') points of view on research. Now let's get practical and think about the ways we should use research in brand building and what types of research we should use.

First of all though, here are our two prejudices about researching when you are thinking of creating a brand or you want to review your brand:

1 Do research among your own staff first. They often know more than your customers can tell you about what's wrong or right, or what you should or should not do.

An international computer company asked their employees what was likely to happen with new product and service ideas, then compared that with what their customer research predicted? Guess who was closest to predicting it accurately. Yup, the employees.

2 Do observational or "ethnographic" research before you do anything else.

This research involves spending time with your customers or potential customers experiencing what they experience or watching how they actually behave in real life.

This gives you extremely valuable insights into what actually happens or could happen to your brand. Nick Durant, whose company Plot provides ethnographic studies for businesses says: "Surveys are about addressing one question to thousands of people; ethnography is about addressing one person with thousands of questions…".

Here are the types of research on offer and when's the best way of using them.

(We're particularly grateful here to Nick and to Martin Lee of the Consultancy Acacia Avenue for his insight.)

Type of research	What it is	What it's best for	When to use it	The problem is
Quantitive surveys	Questionnaires conducted with consumers on the street, via phone or now over the Web	Snapshots of opinions at a given moment in time	At the start of your brand development process if you are trying to get a snapshot of trends in the market	It's only worth doing if you are going to do it properly – i.e. big numbers (thousands)
	On the street should be the most random	"Substantiating" qualitative findings (see below)	At the end if you are trying to evaluate the potential size of the market	The data is quickly dated – which is why it's good for snapshots but not for long-term decision making
	Phone and web are probably better for "targeting"	Identifying trends	And ongoing to understand how well or not you are actually doing	If it's a rainy day on a boring high street, researchers get really depressed and start questioning what the point of their life is
	Usually last 15–20 minutes, characterised by 'closed' questions, i.e. ones you answer yes or no to or give multiple choice answers	Identifying the likely size of groups of target audiences		

Type of research	What it is	What it's best for	When to use it	The problem is
Qualitative surveys – focus groups	Small groups (usually 6–8 people) brought together to discuss a specific topic, usually last a couple of hours and the discussions are led by an independent moderator	In-depth understanding of the reasons behind the qualitative numbers Insights into behaviours and attitudes of consumers Understanding of how different types of consumers might interact Idea generation	You can use it throughout the brand development process to get insight and ideas, rich feedback on the concepts that you are developing And ongoing to understand why you are or are not doing well	They're for insight only – they're not to be used to prove anything statistically Focus group effect happens – where one or two people in the group dominate and skew opinions You get professional focus group attendees – people who seem to turn up at the same groups over and over again They're an artificial environment so they're good for telling you what people think they do

| Qualitative surveys – depth interviews | One-on-one interviews between researcher and consumer – usually lasting an hour and characterised by "open" questions (i.e. "how do you feel about") with no multiple choice answers. Can be done in person, by phone, and via email | In-depth understanding of the reasons behind the qualitative numbers Insights into behaviours and attitudes of consumers | You can use it throughout the brand development process to get insight and ideas, rich feedback on the concepts that you are developing And ongoing to understand why you are or are not doing well | but are not good at showing you what they really do Again, they're neither gospel truth nor statistical proof |

Type of research	What it is	What it's best for	When to use it	The problem is
Mystery shopping	Researchers pretend to be real customers and try buying your product or experiencing your service and feedback	In-depth understanding of what is happening in real life	You can use it when you are thinking about how to improve your existing brand or benchmark against another brand's experience	A lot of staff are now sensitised to mystery shoppers and can often see them coming a mile away which means that they will adjust their behaviour artificially
		Can give you quick real-time feedback that you can respond to if you want		Too often the time taken between when the research is conducted, reported back and any action is taken is too long
		Can pinpoint specific improvements or opportunities		
		Can be used to reward or reprimand staff who outperform or underperform		
Ethnographic studies	Researchers observe customers in real-life situations as they either buy or use the product or service	Brilliant – but then we are biased – at getting real-life, real-world insight into what is actually	Throughout the brand process but especially when you are trying to find ideas to improve or	Best when someone who actually works for you does it, in fact you should do this yourself

	This can include: ■ accompanying shopping trips ■ watching people ■ putting cameras in their houses ■ living with them for a week ■ asking customers to keep diaries, video diaries, etc.	happening and why it is happening Feedback can be fast, continuous and also really interesting (not a boring PowerPoint fest)	opportunities to create a new brand or initiative	Prejudices against it as a bit unscientific
Your own intuition	Using your own eyes, ears, humanity, expertise and experience to look at and think about what is happening and what ideas you could have	Sharpens your business sense Keeps you in touch with your consumers Reminds you that you are a person not a marketeer	Everyday	It's hard work doing your job, isn't it? So much easier to hire a research firm that you can blame if it all goes wrong

Of course, we're only giving you the basics here. Within these approaches there are companies who have their own patented methodologies and black-box techniques such as:

- brand trackers;
- C-SATS (Customer Satisfaction Scores);
- E-SATS (Employee Satisfaction Scores);
- net promoter index;
- brand power indices.

And they'll use a variety of jargon-rich terms such as logit, regression analysis, conjoint analysis, bell curves, S-curves, mean index, etc..

But the raw material that they put through their models basically is gained in one of the ways we have listed above. So, on the theory that no matter how good the engine, if it's garbage in, it will be garbage out, you should make sure that you know how they're getting their data.

So here are the main questions you should ask any research agency when they are pitching to you (and ask them again when they are presenting their results to you):

1 Sample: How big? Who exactly? Why?

2 Time frame: How long and when will fieldwork take place? Why?

3 Structure: What topics? What questions? How many closed? What order? Always ask to see the protocol (interview guide, discussion guide or questionnaire).

4 Fieldwork: Who is conducting it? Where?

5 Data collection and reporting: Who and how?

6 Presentation of findings: How, who, when?

Above all, make sure you are absolutely clear on the following:

1 What precisely is the objective of your research?

2 How are you going to use the findings of the research?

3 In what format do you want the research to be reported?

If you are crystal clear on those three things, then you are likely to get some value out of what can otherwise be a long, costly and ultimately pointless exercise at the end of which you'll either ignore the findings or want to sue someone. Which brings us nicely on to lawyers.

Ignorance of the Law excuses no man.

John Selden

CALL IN THE LAWYERS

Here's a good tip. If you want to find out what your competitor's plans for extending their brand portfolio might be, then visit your country's trademarks register and search for their name. You'll soon find out what brand names they own and for what types of goods they have registered them. You'll then be able to make a pretty informed guess about what plans they might have in the near future.

Despite the fact that trademarks are the most powerful weapon in marketing, marketeers really know little about them. It's like an estate agent knowing nothing about property law. You ever heard horror stories of people buying houses only to discover they don't have access to the back lane? Or that the party wall that is falling down is their liability not the neighbours? And the estate agent's attitude seems to be: "Hey! I just sell the houses. I don't need to know anything about who owns which bit of the land on which they're built."

Well, a marketeer not knowing about trademark law is worse than that.

If you are a marketeer, the least you should know is what trademark protection your brand has got. Can you answer the following without phoning a lawyer friend?

1 How many classes of the trademarks register are there?

2 In which classes is your brand name registered?

3 In which countries is it registered or are you applying to register it?

4 Apart from the brand name, what other parts of your brand's identity have you protected as a trademark?

5 Answer true or false to each of the following. You can register as a trademark a:

(a) logo TRUE or FALSE?

(b) colour TRUE or FALSE?

(c) product design TRUE or FALSE?

(d) slogan TRUE or FALSE?

(e) piece of music TRUE or FALSE?

(f) smell TRUE or FALSE?

(g) hot air TRUE or FALSE?

(We'll give you the answers at the end of this chapter.)

We've met some brand owners whose eyes glaze over when you talk to them about trademark protection, about intellectual property rights. And these same people's eyes would bulge out of their sockets if they were told that they could not extend their brand into a new country because someone else had already got a confusingly similar trademark there, or that they couldn't prevent someone from "borrowing" their brand dress because their brand identity was not sufficiently distinctive to be protected by law.

Remember we said that the reason everyone has brands is for long-term money? Well, trademark protection is what ring-fences that money, it makes sure that

Trademark protection makes sure that the goodwill you build up in your brand gets converted into cash in your bank account and no one else's

the goodwill you build up in your brand gets converted into cash in your bank account and no one else's.

If you do not have a properly protected trademark and a strategy for managing your intellectual property, you do not have a brand in any meaningful sense of the word. It's a bit like having a house that squatters can live in. For free. At your expense. And you still end up mowing the garden.

If you are serious about brand building, you should have an intellectual property (IP) or trademark (TM) lawyer riding shotgun with you on your brand wagon.

In fact, we take our own advice so seriously that we asked one of the best TM lawyers we know, Allan Poulter of Field Fisher Waterhouse, a leading law practice with IP specialism, to check through the rest of this to make sure what we were saying about the relevant laws was correct.

There are millions of registered trademarks in the world. And tens of thousands are being added every day

Here's a fact that might alarm you:

There are millions of registered trademarks in the world. And tens of thousands are being added every day.

So finding a new brand name is tough.

Here is a fun story about trademark misuse:

Volvo discovered that there was a [ahem] gentleman's club in Hong Kong called Club Volvo. They could not do anything about it, under trademark law, because Volvo had never registered their trademark for entertainment services.

The thing was, if the customers weren't guaranteed a very safe and comfortable experience then *that* could have been seriously damaging to the brand. I mean imagine getting that one confused: "Darling, will you drop the kids off in the Volvo ...", etc.. So instead, Volvo were able to plead damage to reputation.

So here are some key tips for protecting your trademarks.

When creating a new brand you should do the following:

1 Get your trademark lawyer to give you his/her advice from the start. Share with them your brand plans and ambitions, including the markets you might consider going into in 5 or 10 years' time. Think about Virgin. It started out selling records, now it's also a bank. Along the way it's sold phones, seats on planes and trains, soft drinks, health and fitness and even bridal wear. That's at least seven different trademark classes in which it would have to register itself.

2 Choose the most distinctive brand name you can. Better that a few people have a short-term giggle at the fact that you're called Zeneca than that you have a long-term problem of no protectable trademark in the world.

3 Registering the brand name is not enough; choose a distinctive logo, trade dress, packaging, etc..

- Nescafé realised that it was easy for supermarkets to copy their colours (brown for standard, gold for premium) and their jars (standard shaped), so they created a distinctive jar shape, which required investment in tooling that no supermarket was going to make.

- Coca-Cola did the same in 1915. They got fed up with bottlers whacking brown fizzy syrup in any kind of bottle and passing it off as the real thing. So they created a very distinctive bottle shape, the one we all know and love today. All their bottlers had to invest in new machinery to make this common, distinctive shaped bottle. Apparently when Coca-Cola announced what it was doing at a bottlers' conference, there was outrage: "You expect us to put up all this money to build new machinery to make your bottles?" Coca-Cola's response was along the lines of "Do it, or we'll see you in court". Guess what? They did it. And still do. Always. And the Coca-Cola bottle shape is a registered trademark too.

4 Don't kid yourself that because you have slapped a TM on something you have got trademark protection. You need to see the glorious ® sign before you know your brand name, logo, and image, shape, colour, whatever has been accepted into the heavenly list of *registered trademarks*. TM indicates you are claiming it just as a trademark. You can use the TM symbol even if you have not applied to register the name as a trademark. ® means you've got it registered. And don't use the ® if your name is not registered – that is a criminal offence and can land you in court!

5 Aggressively protect your rights. If you see anyone attempting to copy your brand or planning to infringe your rights, act swiftly. If you don't contact them quickly telling them you object or

politely pointing out their obviously unintended error then you might undermine, or even lose, your own rights. But don't issue a threatening letter without first taking advice from a trademark lawyer, someone like Allan, or you might find yourself on the wrong side of an "unjustifiable threat" action!

6 Stop people using your brand name as a proxy for the generic product – some personal stereos are Sony Walkman Personal Stereos, not all personal stereos are Walkmen. In fact, Sony lost their rights to the registration of the trademark Walkman in Austria a few years back because the local courts deemed the name to have become a generic! Did you know Sellotape is a trademark? But how many of us ask for Sellotape whenever we mean "sticky back" and do not get a Sellotape brand? You and I might think that's funny, but if you had laboured to invent, patent and market Sellotape for the benefit of the world, how would you feel when copycats come along and steal your name?

7 If you've got the muscle, send people out to shops and bars and see if people are given a competitor's alternative when they have asked for your brand. Some brand owners do this; they send out mystery shoppers to check that "brand substitution" is not happening. We know it sounds a bit Gestapo-like but, if someone comes into a pub and asks for a Coke, he should be given a Coke, not a Pepsi. That's fair, isn't it? If we want to buy a Hoover vacuum cleaner, we want a Hoover, not an Electrolux vacuum cleaner. Nor a Dyson. Hold on. Actually, we think we'd like a Dyson because they are really cool and, remember, they gave Jon great service.

8 If you can't get someone for a direct trademark infringement, get them for passing off. Having a registered trademark means

that, if someone comes along in the same category as you with the same or similar name, it's easier for you to kick their brand out of court. But, even if you can't get them on infringing your trademark registration, then you can try and get them for passing off. That's when:

- someone uses branding similar to yours;
- there is likely to be confusion (even unintentional) in the consumer's mind;
- there is damage to your reputation or business as a result.

Passing off is harder and more expensive to prove, but worth doing to protect your rights.

9 Be aware of the dangers of being seen as a big brand Nazi. For example, Burger King had to take action against a small restaurant in Yorkshire, England, which offered a special meal deal on Sundays for families, called a Family Feast. Unfortunately, Burger King also offers a Family Feast and they have trademark rights in the name Family Feast. So Burger King told the restaurant to cease and desist from using the name. Well, of course, to the outside world, that can be seen as a big guy coming down on a little guy. But it's a dilemma for the big brand owner, because they have to apply the law equally to every company, big or small. If they don't object to a small business using their trademarks, then they won't be able to object to a big business using them. Often a way round this is to apply some common sense and, if you are the big guy, some magnanimity. Offer to come to some licensed-use arrangement or some other form of specific and limited commercial arrangement. Or even offer out of the goodness of your corporate heart to help with the relatively low costs of the small company having to find a new name.

10 Look at all the other forms of intellectual property you have – patents, copyrights, designs and the terms of franchise or distribution agreements, etc. Manage them in a coordinated way. And use them.

If you get any of this stuff wrong, it can cost you millions. So it is best to take a bit of time and get it right.

By the way, searching and registering names or logos can be an expensive business. Often there will be a charge per name or logo searched per class per country. So, if you have a shortlist of 10 names and you intend to launch your brand in 10 countries and you have to search it in 2 classes, that's 200 × £*X*. So here are some good tips for saving money (if you have the time) when you are searching for a new brand name:

- Search your list of names first against identical trademarks in the main markets you are interested in and for existing domain names.
- Then conduct full searches (i.e. looking for similar names) against the survivors in the main or key countries in which you will launch, e.g. the UK or USA.
- Then take the surviving names on to the next country, and so on.

It can add a few weeks to the process but, the more you can stage the process, the more money you will save.

The same applies to registering the names. In some countries you have to file a separate application for each class of the trademark register that you have to be in and you will be charged for each application. So, if you are Virgin, there might be some countries where you have to file once for airlines, once for soft drinks, once for music, etc. Thankfully, most countries are moving to multi-use applications, i.e. you pay for only one filing and a smaller additional cost for each trademark class.

And this is just the basics, by the way. If you really want to manage your trademark portfolio properly, then you should also look at how to manage them tax efficiently. That means deciding in which country you should assign the original registration of the brand and to which company. For example, brands like Kit Kat and Maltesers, which are popular chocolate brands in the UK, are owned by a Swiss company, Nestlé, who licenses out the use of the trademarks to its UK registered operating company. That way, part of the profits on each sale of each brand gets taxed only at Swiss rates, not at UK rates. And that once represented a big saving!

So it's important stuff, this trademark management. And it is only going to get more important as fewer and fewer companies actually make anything tangible and more and more own intangibles. Apple doesn't position itself as a manufacturer of products, it lets us know that they are "designed in California" because the design and the branding is so important. Nike is seen primarily as a product design and marketing company not a manufacturing business. Google and Yahoo don't "make" anything at all and much of what appears on MySpace or YouTube is "user-generated content", i.e. stuff "made" by people like you and me.

The lesson is: trademark lawyers are important. And if you want good advice in the field of trademark law then speak to Allan and his colleagues at www.ffw.com, they'll help you.

Oh, and here are the answers to our quiz.

1 45

2 How should we know? Check the list of classes we've given you in the Appendix and make your own mind up.

3 Ditto. The classes are nearly the same in every country, though.

4 Stop expecting us to know the answers! It's your brand!

5 **(a)** TRUE (Golden Arches of McDonald's, Nike's swoosh, to name but two of thousands).

   (b) TRUE (Cadbury's own purple as a trademark for use on chocolate and the colour orange is protected for telecommunication companies by, erm, Orange).

   (c) TRUE (Coke bottle, Mini car design, etc.).

   (d) TRUE ("That'll do Nicely!").

   (e) TRUE (Intel's sound signature is theirs to keep!).

   (f) TRUE (there are trademark registrations for the smell of plumeria blossom for thread and one for the smell of roses on tyres – yup, not kidding, only one brand's tyres – by law! – can smell like that).

   (g) FALSE (or possibly a trick question, if your brand name is Hot Air and you have registered it for something other than air conditioning or hairdryers).

"

Success has many fathers. Bastards have none.

Anon.

"

BOW TIES, PONYTAILS AND LUNCH AT THE IVY

How to manage your agencies

The secret to creating a great brand identity or a great brand campaign is first to pick the right people (designers or ad agency) for you. You need to be able to trust the people creating your brand with you – this doesn't mean roll over, you should still input – but you don't buy a dog and bark yourself – especially if it's an expensive dog – so get your money's worth.

To do this well, you have to:

1 understand the different type of agency you need for each task;

2 manage the pitch properly so you can choose the right one;

3 understand and manage as a team the agencies you have chosen in order to get the best work out of them;

4 understand and agree the key principles that will determine the success of a great campaign.

Choosing the type of agency you need

First of all, understand what type of advice you are buying. A brand consultancy, an advertising agency, a digital agency or new media or live experience agency?

It's getting increasingly hard to tell what type of agency you are working with, as the trend has been to integrate disciplines or buy teams of people from other backgrounds. But, if you're working with the local shop or the big league big boys you ought to be able to tell their main area of business. Everyone will talk about brand. The brand consultancies should be able to explain the idea behind the business, not just the campaign.

The ad agency will have a great portfolio of, well, ads – so probably they're the easiest to work out. Digital agencies will focus on the web and live agencies will have a lot of work focused on events and launches. It helps to know what area of focus the company you are working with has – and if you are a client you will get more out of the agency if you are basically asking them to do more of what they do best. The difference will be experience, focus and approach.

Whilst speaking recently with a very hot executive creative director of a boiling hot ad agency (one cleaning up at the D&AD awards) we briefly discussed "What is the difference in the purpose of what design and advertising agencies do?". The answer – is f*** all. They both help build brands. The difference is in what they are credible in offering. Branding, like any creative industry, is what you could describe as "t-shaped". That is to say, it spans wide and goes deep. As wide and as deep as you like. It's a bit wanky to say to someone that you are an "ideas man", so you say what that person, be they a cabby, dinner party guest or client, understands, e.g. "I work in marketing, in advertising, etc.'. It's human nature to want simplicity and to want to label everything. Hey, corporate identity sounds good, let's call it that. Er, nope, you've just designed a logo. Branding sounds like we could charge more money for it. Hang on a minute, isn't that a logo?, etc. So if you reveal or present a logo or a piece of film, then call it what it is, don't pretend it's advertising, branding, corporate identity or quantum brandchanics. That's spin or, at best, a bit of a laugh.

So here's some help for you to decode the *brand speak* – what they are saying and what they are selling:

Brand – advert, if advertising agency

Brand – logo, if design agency

Brand – centrally driving idea, if a brand consultancy

Brand – product, if a client

Brand – strapline, if a copywriter

Brand – personality, if a promotions agency

Brand – space, if an environments agency

Brand – reputation, if a PR agency

And so it goes on. Another way of spotting their difference and understanding what they really do is the "triangle test". Often they will spontaneously present or draw on a flip chart a triangle which shows their "view of branding" – this will show you what their real specialism is. If they don't do this, you can always be a bit cheeky and ask them, "If you were drawing me a picture of how you view brands, how would you do it?" and ask them to draw you one.

Anyway, it's important to know what you're getting. Put it this way: you don't go to a hip replacement specialist if you need rhinoplasty but both would probably tell you they are in the health sector.

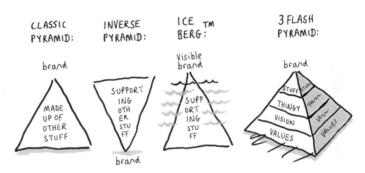

HOW TO SKIN A TRIANGLE. . . .

How to get the best out of the pitch

Once you know what type of agency you are looking for (i.e. if you want to send mailshots across the UK, then get a direct mail agency, or brand-response agency as they are sometimes called, don't waste your time asking for a full-service advertising agency). Follow these tips on which one to select:

1 Be clear about what you want. Think about it as if you were buying a house, so location, key services, national/international, established/new, fees/commision, etc. should be at the core of your shortlist.

2 Be clear about who you want. You are actually buying people and relationships, particularly as most work that is presented and even wins the pitch to the client does not end up being the work that is actually shown to the consumer on TV. Ensure you understand the culture of the agency, even meet the people socially (do you get on?). Look at their work beyond the showcase highlights and see if it fits your brand, because you will get more of the same. When you meet the agency team, mentally remove the most impressive person, what are you left with? Repeat the process – this will give a strong clue as to the strength and depth of your team.

3 Have a process that maximises your chances of finding the right partner. Having too many pitching agencies will dilute the time you can spend with the participants. Three to five agencies pitching is probably ideal. Make sure agencies have access to key decision makers and influencers. 270 questions for a request for information (RFI) or request for proposal (RFP) are morale sapping and rarely relevant – what do you really need to know? Have a timetable and adhere to it. Be prepared for news of the

pitch to leak – either take pre-emptive action and announce it or be ready for the inevitable leak. Offer a debrief to losing agencies.

4 Be honest with an incumbent. What are their chances, and what is your willingness to re-appoint?

5 Make sure that your team is fully prepared. Ensure you make yourself available to meet agencies, answer questions, and discuss/decide internally on key decision criteria.

How to get the best out of the agency's work

Once you have selected the right company, you have a duty to get the best work from them. You do this in two ways:

1 how you treat each individual agency;

2 how you understand them as a team.

1 How you treat each individual agency

(a) **Be clear about the work/brief**.
This includes the budget, timetable, process, etc. This should prevent wasted time and energy. Clear briefing is a skill. So is making a simple point. As Churchill made the point when apologising for a long speech, "I didn't have the time to write a shorter one." Clarity is king in managing business and accounts.

(b) **The power of "yes"**.
Let them know who has the final authority to say yes to a proposal – too many ideas get massacred by people with influence but without authority.

(c) Know when and how to say no.

If an idea isn't right or is going nowhere, a "no – start again" is far better than avoiding the issue. But make sure it's a positive no to re-engender motivation.

(d) Keep rechecking everything with the agency.

This includes the quality of the strategy, the (creative) idea and the execution. We bet everyone's Dad used to say, "You've got two ears and one mouth. Use them in that order." Listening to what people say is key to avoiding going over and over the same old ground.

(e) Agencies work best for clients whom they find rewarding and enjoyable

A thank you/well done to an individual/team goes a very long way. Ask for regular updates on the agency; be as interested in their fortunes as they are in yours. Have regular mutual feedback – identify and improve how and what you do.

2 How you understand them as a team

(a) Understand egos and politics.

It makes us laugh when we hear people in our industry say: "There's no politics where I work." Unfortunately, there are egos everywhere and, in the design, advertising or media industries, the egos are huge, ginormous – why else do you think these guys need such big cars, houses or offices? To fit all those egos in! Ha ha. If you can keep the world in perspective, not get depressed or have a nervous breakdown, then it can be the best job in the world.

Resist the power of the forceful argument of one ego. There was once a very senior figure in the branding industry, who, when at the point of losing an argument about a (pretty big global) brand, declared: "Well, f*** it, let's just launch it and see what happens." Fortunately for him, this was laughed off as him being a bit "crazy". Unfortunately, we knew he was serious. Large corporations might be able to get away with the "Brewsters' Millions" approach to some Midas-powered superbrands like Nike, Coke or SuperSuperDoggyPants.com, but mere mortals can't, however big their egos.

(b) Don't be fooled by the "we're all part of a global network" sales pitch.
These days, most big ad agencies, design companies and brand consultancies are all owned worldwide by three or four big players. The chances are that, if you start to work with one of these as a client, you may be introduced into the wider network.

However, don't expect the companies to get on. Often two similar agencies in the same group will nick each other's staff and compete against each other. Most young designers want to work for an ad agency. A lot of ad agency people fancy them-selves as the brand owners, and like the idea of being strategists. Ad guys hate consultants thinking they own the relationship with the client. Consultants are the ones that have put brand on the boardroom agenda, and that's one of the reasons why the big ad groups like WPP or Omnicom own brand agencies – as the way in to the client.

(c) Understand that the different types of agencies may not get on.
It's quite naive to think that different creative businesses will get along. Brand boys hate the crudeness of advertising (and lack of kerning). Jon once had an ad agency executive tell him he had

got the "leading" (pronounced "ledding" and means line spacing) wrong on a single line logotype. He was amused by this, especially as they meant the weight of the type. They thought that it was too heavy (like a lead weight). Ad guys hate brand creatives who apparently don't get advertising – mostly because they don't get it, and try to write ads that "sound" like ads (punning, etc.) rather than communicate the proposition. Or often, if they don't use *lorem ipsum* (Greek words in the place of copy), they will use one-word headlines. This irritates ad agencies.

There have been a few recent public spats between brand consultancies and advertising agencies. It strikes us that, actually, advertising is arrogant but confident and sure about what it does. Advertising is bigger, has been established for longer and has not kept changing the name of what it does. The design industry, for the most part, is more defensive about its position. You can see why a guy responsible for million-pound accounts may not want to listen to someone he thinks worries about the kerning on the back of the biscuit pack. Similarly, the design-obsessed can't seem to see the bigger picture and will accuse those not kerning-obsessed of being "commercial".

Now, we've played both sides of the coin – having worked in and with the biscuit brigade and played with the global big boys. There are no answers here, and whatever the two disciplines are called – where there's money involved and more than one company vying for a share – there will be complications.

(d) Clarify roles and responsibilities and establish common goals and *esprit de corps*.

It's good to get focus and clarity of responsibilities within the teams of your agencies, and within the roles of agencies if you have a multi-agency/multi-disciplinary team. Invest time in this. Take all the agency teams away for a couple of days somewhere. Somewhere nice too. Rebrief them as one. Play games that get them to introduce each other and understand each other. Walk on hot coals. Do transcendental meditation or just get them drunk, whatever works for you and the team. But do something that creates a shared experience and forms a common bond. And follow up every few months with a good meal in a restaurant at the end of a formal review of "how we're doing".

Don't design ads with one-word headlines – unless you like a good argument

So if you missed all that:

1 Try and remember you're all on the same team.

2 If you're a client, have an opinion – but be ready to be compelled.

3 Make it clear who is presenting work and who is critiquing work.

4 Don't design ads with one-word headlines – unless you like a good argument.

5 Never book the restaurant in your name, always use the ad agency's name (and make sure they pay and don't charge it back plus a 10 per cent handling fee).

Understand and agree the principles that will make a great campaign

We've not gone into detail on these because each campaign is special for each brand but these are the main principles you must address if you want to make sure the campaign will work.

Be ruthlessly single-minded in your campaign message to your target audience

A great brand advertising campaign is different from managing the brand as a whole. The overall management and building of your brand involves multiple stakeholders, different touch-points and often different people and you often have to use different but related messages, styles, etc. In a campaign you have to be laser-like in your focus on what you want your target audience to do and therefore what is the message they need to hear. The briefer, the simpler that message is and the tighter and more focused you are on who the target audience is, the better. For example, say you were running a campaign on road safety. An ineffective brief would be: "Raise general awareness among people that there are a number of ways in which their safety on roads can be compromised and also that they can themselves contribute to the deaths or injuries of others. At the same time, ensure people are aware that there are different degrees of punishment for traffic offences." A good brief would be: "Make dangerous drivers understand that they ruin lives, including their own."

Understand your target audience's 24/7 360 media consumption

24/7 360 media is an ugly bit of jargon for which we apologise. It means that all day, every day and all around them there are countless media touchpoints that your target audience will interact with in some way, some of which you might not even have considered as a medium for your message. Of course there's TV, radio, newspapers, web but there's also the staircase in a tube station, including the steps themselves, gyms, the handlebars of the exercise bike in the gyms, etc. You need to find out how your audience live their lives and when they are at the most receptive to your message and through which media. One of our favourite media now is the consumer's own body on which he or she might even tattoo your logo if it's cool enough. Some Harley Davidson bikers do.

Connect everything

The power of any campaign is in the way that you cumulatively build the message by connecting each touchpoint consistently. Don't run wildly different campaigns, looks, logos, images, etc. at different touchpoints. Let them all connect. For example, when Sony PlayStation launched their Society Against PlayStation campaign, not only did the ads spoof parents trying to stop their kids playing the game but the stores had zones where people weren't supposed to go but where the PlayStations were.

Dial up and dial down

In some media you need to shout loud and in some media you need to be subtle. In some media you can tease and hint at your brand's identity and in others you need to be "in their face". A good agency will advise you on which.

Be bold and relentless

Once you have an idea, be bold with it and relentless in its execution. Take the Nestlé Yorkie chocolate bar campaign in the UK a few years ago. They decided to reinvent a failing chunky chocolate bar, which was associated with an outdated masculine image, into a post-modern cheeky lad's treat. They're "it's not for girls" campaign ran everywhere, including a special logo of a woman inside a red "stop" symbol in the "o" of the brand name Yorkie on the pack, trial samples being handed out in the streets to men only and a Web-based quiz to gauge how much of a "bloke" you were. It could have been offensively sexist but was so clearly and unashamedly "tongue in cheek" that even women loved it.

One last word of warning

Finally, if you're redoing work or rebranding, or just embarking on another piece of work, then beware the "brand plumbers". Not to be confused with branders that used to be plumbers (although this is feasible). You'll recognise the "brand plumbers" first by the sharp intake of breath or teeth sucking that happens when we see the existing work or idea. Second, by the phrase: "Who put this in for you last time then?" Or, "Good job we turned up when we did to tear out all the bad architecture and inner-workings of your brand to replace it with new stuff." Of course, the brand plumber probably "doesn't have the tools in the van" to fix this for you straight away. It'll definitely need another quote or estimate.

Some people might think this sounds like hard work. Well, it is. But it's also fun and you're a privileged person if you're paid for doing something that is fun. And if you do all this, you'll get a great result (more often than not!). And, anyway, it is your job. So get on with it.

"

There are three rules in branding: differentiate, differentiate, differentiate.

Roberto Goizetta, former chairman of the Coca-Cola Company

STANDING UP, STANDING OUT AND STANDING ON YOUR COMPETITION

How to keep your brand fresh in the "Noo Meejur" digital age

*10

Since the marketing-led 1970s and ad-busting 1980s, the desire to be different has been on the agenda of business. We've had the unique selling point (USP) and the point of difference (POD). Old-school marketeers, perhaps those of the Kotler persuasion, still hold onto tracking down these elusive differences. More modern branding era strategists talk about a "differentiator". In the mandatory 2 × 2 matrix that will be drawn up to understand a basic marketing position, the gap (usually top right) that is left allows a convenient position of "difference" to be understood. Differences are to be protected, it is assumed, and this allows some elements, graphics, logos or other assets, to be registered. Difference can be a powerful asset, but it's probably worth working out the role of difference in your business – if you can understand that, then it is very powerful. That way you won't be chasing differences for the sake of it.

The real difference will be understood as a simple thing that resonates with the customer (Orange and billing per second) or the distinctive look of a product (the Dyson vacuum cleaner). Arguably, the real difference in a brand is the sum of its parts, and, if you examine it, the "differentiator" will be an epitome of the brand attitude. Difference is how brands stand out against the competition, but it needs to be earned.

Maybe a good place to start with understanding difference is the desire to do things better. If your business can genuinely claim that the way you do things is driven by a desire to make things better – then it will be different by default. Better forces you to improve, to not settle for what it is you do – to innovate, to be creative.

By considering "better" rather than just "different" as a goal, perhaps you can look at your business in a way that starts to unravel the truth behind what you do.

By considering "better" rather than just "different" as a goal, perhaps you can look at your business in a way that starts to unravel the truth behind what you do.

We've been to so many work-shops where clients and agency people alike obsess around what it is that is "different" about what the business does. However, "better" is better as it forces you to think about your role in the world.

By holding onto being "different" for difference sake, you are effectively sticking in the old-school mentality, as this suggests that you would seek to protect, defend and presumably guide-line how your brand is different. Brands with a cause or a genuine desire to be better than what has gone before are ahead of their time.

Since the mid-1990s businesses and agencies (mostly agencies trying to get their head around it) have been talking about sus-tainability and often, in the same breath, corporate and social responsibility (CSR). Environmental issues globally have become more than a passing trend and have now spearheaded the interest of the general public to delve deeper into what are the CSR policies or actions of the businesses, banks, petrol sta-tions, shoe companies, what you will – brands they use and buy into. At the same time, for the last 15 to 20 years we inevitably have been funnelled into a brand backlash. With seemingly everyone telling you about what they "believe in", what was once a powerful brand standpoint has become more of a hygiene factor with brands. The convergence of CSR/sustainability with the overuse of branding has meant that today's and, even more so, tomorrow's brands have to do more than state their values. They have to live the brand and demonstrate what they stand for. On a heavy level this means that organic brands have to be organic, banks shouldn't invest in politically unstable countries and t-shirt makers shouldn't exploit Third World workers. On a lighter note, living the brand can be more fun, and brands can have the licence to entertain if that format fits with and is a clever extension of their personality.

Brand used to be what a business stood for but it is now also what it stands up and is counted for. As the market places more pressure on each brand to do what it says it does, some brands are leading the way by creating more innovative sponsorships, ambient media or entertainment.

Stella Artois successfully sponsored films on Channel 4, but, cleverer still, was one of the first to sponsor outdoor cinema in the summer. Taking its image away from the pub and "footy Saturdays" and transforming it into a world of picnic blankets and hampers, how civilised.

Back in 2001, BMW was one of the first brands to embrace the power of actually making long films for entertainment. Available virally on the web, and distributed by DVD to select customers, BMW involved top action directors such as Ang Lee and Guy Richie with then wife Madonna in one particular starring role along with Clive Owen as the driver in a series of action shorts. The first batch of films were reported to have cost $15 million – small fry to a brand that would spend a lot more making and placing a TV campaign.

Living the brand in sponsorship

Businesses that are brand-led open themselves up so much more than just products or services or "desirable images". They can be platforms for entertainment. Sponsorship of things like football or Formula One is not a new idea. Before current legislation came in, most Formula One sponsorship was blanketed by the cigarette manufacturers, clustering together like estate agents on a high street. Associating themselves with glamour and getting the bang for buck in terms of television coverage that such sponsorship gives. Similarly football and cricket have been heavily sponsored by telecoms and technology companies. Familiarity makes the brands seem big and powerful, which leads to a perception of trust among consumers.

In more modern times though, sponsorship strategies are cleverer. Red Bull is a brilliant example of a brand that has understood entertainment and picked perfect sponsorship collaborations, having decided to carve itself out as the quintessential energy drink that "revitalises body and mind". Its Flugtag (named subtly to remind you of its Austrian heritage) event is a great way to bring communities together and provide a fun day out for all the family. The idea is that teams of people build craft to see how far they can "fly" into the Serpentine – an artificial lake in London's Hyde Park. These localised events provide an easy way into the brand, supporting the fun characteristics and upbeat values of the brand, whilst reminding you of the idea that "Red Bull gives you wings™". Most clever of all is that this frivolity feels as on-brand and part of the character as the more serious Red Bull Air Races. These worldwide events at glamorous locations are paid-for ticket events. By creating the "World Series" these events create more than a sponsorship: they become their own premier league. Televised around the world, these events make Red Bull synonymous with high-octane fun, daring, skill and concentration. The brand idea of "wings" is perfectly executed. Red Bull also sponsors Formula One, the latest cars cheekily writing "gives you wings" on the rear wing of the car.

They were also one of the first sponsors to involve changing the way sponsorship of Formula One cars worked by placing small photographs of people or consumers that had bought tiny bits of space on the car. This sort of thinking challenges the status quo and is a bit of fun.

In many countries, festivals are used by brands to bring communities together, showing the behaviour of the brand whilst enforcing its offer. Such festivals can even evolve into the modern equivalent of a "village fête" that brings brands into the community and the community together under the brand. Fruitstock is one such event, local to London, that innocent drinks, a smoothie manufacturer, holds in places such as Regent's Park in the summer. Normally a free event, this gets everyone drinking the product and chilling out listening to bands. It is a clever way of enhancing the natural aspect of the drinks, but also serves to reinforce the legend of innocent's conception, by young entrepreneurs that sold their first drinks at a festival.

O_2, the UK telecoms brand, put a big stake in the ground by buying the former Millenium Dome in Greenwich, South East London, and renaming it to the O_2. Apart from the apparent odd few people who turn up to the O_2 shopping centre in Finchley Road (North London and no relation to the telco), people flock to the Greenwich venue, which is thriving with its bars and cinemas. It is as popular a venue for live concerts as Wembley Stadium. The public have no problem referring to the building as the O_2 – in fact it signifies how old you are if you still refer to it as the Dome. This is a clever way of O_2 penetrating a young audience that is into information, communication and entertainment (ICE). By giving priority and deals to customers that want to book events it gives a relevant and strong incentive to be part of the brand. It is a clever way of covering its credibility with the younger part of its broad demographic too. A strategy upheld by its Wireless event which it holds in London's Hyde Park, yearly.

Wireless is a branding device, similar to innocent drinks' Fruitstock in that it puts the masterbrand a little to the side so it's not rammed down the punter's throat. But, like Fruitstock, Wireless reminds the punters of O_2's apparent cutting-edge credibility. Unlike Fruitstock, Wireless is a chargeable festival, but offers special discounts to O_2 customers. Like the Red Bull Air Race, it proves that fans of sports, music and any other pursuit, not just brand affiliates, will pay to live your brand.

Let's get digital, digital (to the tune of Olivia Newton-John's 1983 hit "Physical")

Business is full of buzzwords and digital has become the buzzword of choice, up there with the old favourites brand and strategy. So say hello to "digital brand strategies" with clients asking if they should "do a viral" at the top of the agenda. It's worth pointing out that, if you want to be streetwise and cool, digital is passé and, in fact, "time-based" is the way forward. We've invented time-based media strategies, as time covers all known media and cannot be superseded. You read about it here first, folks!

So what's the big fuss about digital? Did your grandparents once exclaim in wonderment that "everything is done on computers" – because it was? Well, digital is like that. Pretty much all advertising, design and film is produced digitally. And pure digital is work that uses the Web. Traditional advertising, i.e. prime-time television, outdoor sites and press, consumes vast marketing budgets, so the Web has come into its own as a relatively low-cost option.

By creating your own website, as a client, you can measure awareness, popularity of subjects, and update the information you supply, instantly. The dot.com boom of the 1990s saw online brands created for the sake of it but now, for a lot of retail brands, their online presence is booming with a purpose. The web has become the new telly, as people Google-hop or check out Facebook, in a similar way that we channel-hopped the TV. With a lot of Internet hero brands, such as eBay, apparently invented by accident, digital brands can have a much greater sense of sincerity than their traditional TV channel advertising-driven counterparts.

Websites have become much freer and unexpected, full of film and multimedia, downloads and links. The Web still emulates our learned behaviours from television, meaning it's often not relevant now whether you are watching something via the web or on your TV. In technology there is a trend that has been evolving towards singularity – or the "convergence" of disciplines. As communications evolve the same is true. The ATL, BTL and TTL (above, below and through the line) strategies merge into one along with digital and online strategies. The brand sits at the core and informs the overarching point or idea.

There is still a role for traditional advertising, partly due to inertia and also because of the trust that still resonates from TV coverage. It is a bit premature to start to panic that TV advertising will be over any time soon. Manufacturers such as TiVo have paved the way for the viewer to actively deselect adverts when it is recording channels. Until we are all actively de-screening, though, TV advertising will continue to work harder, to become more engaging and interrupt you in a different way. Perhaps the future of how television advertising will have to evolve lies in how virals have become successful, i.e. being a way of entertaining people rather than overtly "selling" to them.

Isn't viral dangerous?

So what the hell is viral anyway? Viral describes the method of distribution of stuff, usually via email or the internet. In the old pre-digital days we used to call it "word of mouth" recommendation. Virals are things, usually short films, pictures

Even POST-IT notes can be digital

or links to websites, that are passed on from friend to friend. So when you get something that you find funny, rude, good or whatever your definition of entertaining is – then you share it by sending it on to your mates, and they send it to their mates. Pretty soon the thing spreads like a virus.

You could say that virals started as jokes and chain letters, and then evolved into picture attachments (usually rude, stupid, unfortunate or compromising situations – or all of the afore-mentioned). Advertisers cottoned on to this pretty fast and, as people sent entertaining ads to each other, ad agencies made versions or spoof versions that got sent around. Short films were sent as attachments, meaning that the shorter format of adverts (30-second or 60-second spots) were ideally suited. Now, with content-sharing sites such as YouTube that host user-generated content, emails only have to contain a link and can be sent out and onwards easier and faster. Sites such as YouTube mean anyone can be onwards the web – making the internet everyone's potential personal TV station.

The early adopters of user-generated sites embraced the fact that it allowed you to upload anything, so there was a lot of rubbish on the web. There was, however, a new sense of "authenticity" or "realness" of what you could now find. In our opinion, the gems were usually the ridiculous but genuine 'lo-fi' films that people reworked and interacted with. The "*Star Wars* kid" being a brilliant example of how something slightly silly but mundane could be remixed and made hilari-ous. If you haven't seen it, Google or better still YouTube it.

We liked the ridiculousness of "Andy Milonakis", the Greek-American kid whose webcam raps, whines, whinges and rants were about nothing in particular but full of random sickness and the surreal as he attempted to join his raps up with rhyme. His popularity pretty fast earned him his own show on MTV USA. In 2007 we, along with most of the Web, tuned into Tay Zonday's *Chocolate Rain* random song, sung by a young bloke with an exceedingly deep baritone voice. This guy was quickly remixed by Dr Pepper – leading the whole thing to look like a set-up. Looking over the internet, Google and Wikipedia to see if this was a hoax or not doesn't really throw up any evidence. We think it's hilarious that there is so much paranoia about whether things on the Web are "real" or not. The reality is it doesn't matter, as long as it's entertaining.

The double-bluffing emulation of user-generated content is perhaps a pointer to the new rules of engagement for advertising on other media. There's a role for viral and a role for traditional advertising as part of the overall plan. Adverts have parodied themselves on the Web. Brands have lampooned other brands using viral. It seems that virals can behave above the law. It makes it harder to complain about something if you can't define its origin. Virals allow brands to be subversive; they can be more risqué or focused and cult in their segmentation. Whether it's Kylie on a bucking bronco in her Agent Provocateur undies, a Ford Ka getting its own back on cats and pigeons, or kids surfing a dynamited wave in a city river for Quicksilver; viral ads enable the brand to create risqué, dark, sexy or post-watershed entertainment.

The Web can be a great testbed for brands to check out the popularity or relevance of their attitude. Nike and John West

Tuna are great examples of safer (i.e. not offensive or crude) adverts that were so popular on YouTube that they released them on TV.

Virals are popular with advertisers, i.e. clients, not only because they can reach specific demographic audiences, penetrating under the radar, but because of the lack of media spend needed to put them into traditional spaces. Although there are dedicated companies that concentrate on the planning and planting of virals, it's still a method that is extremely hard to predict or control.

The viral method means you are able to poke fun at yourself and show a different side to your brand. Assuming you don't do anything to damage your brand, it is a powerful way to explore how you can evolve and expand your standpoint. Perhaps the biggest point of the internet for brands is the speed of publishing – i.e. its instantaneity and its reach. This has meant that all markets now move much faster. It's easier to track your competition and see what it's up to.

The idea of brand owners latching onto the Web using viral methods is a precursor to how brands are trying to occupy the spaces where we now spend our time. In the first proper virtual reality site that has been open to the Web, Second Life has been populated by brands and services as fast as individuals. Second Life is an interesting concept, particularly as it has its own trading currency. Facebook applications have been one of the latest brand wagons. Brand agencies have been talking about communities ever since the birth of the Web, but it's taken the likes of Facebook for people to really understand networking sites. By piggy-backing the main application, program makers (and therefore, potentially, brand sponsors) have the ability to infiltrate your social space, and get a better understanding of what you really are up to than superstore points cards and loyalty schemes.

Digital stuff that used to be available only on your computer is now available on your mobile phone, with the advent of 3G and the advance of broadband, so that you can take your internet experience with you. Moreover, brands can connect with you via software applications, and now they have the potential to connect with you in specific geographical areas. We can download games or applications that are branded, often the pay-off for being free.

One area of brand management for which it has caused a dilemma is the notion of traditional brand guidelines. When brands have to update and compete at the speed of the internet, the speed of live RSS-fed now-ness, it brings into question how to protect a brand. Guidelines, especially those concerning the visual side of the brand, have become out of date with modern brands. The slow tweak of the Shell or Cadbury marque, evolving over decades, has been challenged by a new breed of brands that look to own an attitude and greater visual manifestation than just their logo. Coca-Cola is a good example of how it brings nostalgia or heritage back into a modern cutting-edge brand. There's the Coke Zone and the World of Coca-Cola that are ever changing and kept up to date. The graphic language of Coke is normally a good barometer of what is contemporary cool. Yet they still manage to retain and utilise the Coke name and the icon of the bottle. Glass bottles exist still to buy, small or large. As do plastic bottles in the same classic shape to remind us of the nostalgic glass bottle experience. And playing with the form and shape iconically and ironically, they have even used the Coke can as a collectable glass in McDonald's. So we are reminded of their heritage, and even cans are made to feel classic and iconic – which is genius. Maybe it's only in car brands such as Porsche that history (or old colours, liveries and identities) are used as a selling point in merchandise and not thrown away. We suppose it's only a matter of time before Apple makes things so small, thin and light that it will bring out a limited edition slow, heavy and low-capacity "nostalgia" model of something.

Google is perhaps the best example of a young brand that has managed to create heritage status in our minds. Google has a really simple identity yet changes and plays with its logo every day. Because it can. Because it is digital and instant and its content is what you decide. That relevant reference to time/news/current affairs lives light-heartedly in its logo changing or adapting. Even Google has managed to create iGoogle now and leave the traditional Google site as its "classic site" still available.

So, by contextualising your brand as heritage there is arguably room to play with your other assets (assuming you don't mind going through registration rights if you want to protect it).

One of our favourite brands is Oliver Goldsmith sunglasses. Amazingly cool. Brilliant story. They have thoroughly understood the need for authenticity, that unique combination of context and heritage. Claire Goldsmith, director of Oliver Goldsmith sunglasses, puts it like this:

in a world of a million brands fighting for attention, Oliver Goldsmith stands out because I think it appeals to people's hearts and imaginations. It conjures up the memory of a time when celebrity was real, aviation was glamorous and going to the cinema was a real night out. When going through the old archives in my uncle's dusty attic and reading the back catalogues stored for 20 years, I fell totally in love with this brand's history and the era in which it emerged. I have tried to retell this story in all its glory in the hope that others will also fall in love with the brand and what it stands for, just as I did.

Anyway, here are our top five tips for standing out:

1 Embrace don't replace.
New technologies and strategies are there to be explored, but it helps if you don't see them as the golden egg that will replace the goose of your existing activity. Look to complement traditional with modern. TV with digital. Print with viral, etc. This is no different to making sure your shopping bag is as relevant as your tactical ad. If you're a client, you'll soon see what's effective and most relevant. If you're agency side, don't be threatened by new alternatives – find out how these can work as complementary and relish the opportunities. Embrace the new.

2 Don't stuff it down people's throats.

You don't have to ram the brand down people's proverbial or real throat. Think about creating sub-branded events like Fruitstock or Wireless that feel community-focused and have the relevant permissions to be there. The key issue being relevance – which can lead to credibility. Also, don't mistake plastering your brand everywhere for stand out. If customers can tell your brand from the people you employ, or the colours that you use, or your way of speaking, in the right context, that is really powerful. Think of the relevant parts of the brand experience where this is most effective – you don't have to irritate by intruding everywhere.

3 Be audacious.

On the other hand, if you are going to do something, be brave and ballsy. O_2 renaming the dome and claiming it as an expression of the brand is a great example of ambition and can-do.

4 Be better not just different.

Remember, in the branding game, different is worth something only if it helps you stand out as being better. Don't obsess with difference, seek out what your cause is and champion it at all costs.

5 Spare some change, buddy.

Change is remorseless, and the friend of progress. The old way of thinking was to be regimented into brand guidelines and, yes, they have their time and place and maybe sectors. Brands that can accommodate a bit of change or evolution can be as powerful as those that remain steadfast. If you're on the way up, aim to build in flexibility. If you're a power brand or brand leader, then think about where you can surprise your customers with positive, new thinking. One way to lead a market is to redefine the rules.

"

Not everything that counts, can be counted and not everything that can be counted, counts.

Albert Einstein

"

HOW TO MEASURE BRAND PERFORMANCE

*11

Return on investment is both a mantra and the holy grail of marketing. As Lord Lever (one of the Lever brothers whose company eventually became Unilever) is famously reported to have said, "I know that half of the money I spend on advertising is wasted, I just don't know which half."

Here's what we believe about measuring brand performance.

Most measures of brand performance actually measure only part of the experience people have of the brand, i.e. awareness image or sales impact.

Even when they do measure factors that determine the experience the consumer or customer is having, usually it is used by the marketing team only to plan a new advertising or sales promotion campaign.

We say that brand is everything you do and everything you say. That's why people buy you and often pay more for you repeatedly. And focusing on those things that help to build desire and loyalty for your brand can save you costs in your organisation. And all that adds up to sustainable and growing profit, to long-term money. (That was Chapter 1, remember?)

So, if what we say is true – and we say it is – then you need a measure of brand performance that looks at your business as a whole, that understands what drives your customers to love you, what are the most effective ways of increasing that love and how all that makes you money (not just drives sales, because, as any marketer will tell you, you can drive a huge number of sales overnight simply by dropping your prices!).

Such a measure exists to understand brand performance and that measure is called brand valuation.

Brand valuation puts a figure on the amount of money you earn as a business and reasonably could be expected to earn in the future. It ties the soft factors of marketing (awareness, preference, advocacy, image, etc.) with the hard factors of finance (earnings before interest and taxes (EBIT), forecast revenues, capital employed, etc.). It makes brand performance an enterprise-wide accountability issue, not just the marketeer's metric!

There are many companies now that offer brand valuation services. If you just type the term brand valuation into your Google search engine, you'll find out about them. But here are the three common principles that underpin brand valuation:

1 What role is demand for your brand actually playing in the reasons people buy you?

Although the brand is everything you do and everything you say as far as you are concerned, people might not like you very much but still might be forced to buy you for other reasons. For example, take petrol stations. You might not like Shell very much, you might prefer BP (or vice versa) but, if your car needs petrol, you are going to fill up at the nearest station regardless of who owns it. Whereas, if you like *Chanel No 5*, you'll buy *Chanel No 5*, you won't just get something to make you smell nice. So "brand preference" is less important in the petroleum industry than, by comparison, it is in the perfume industry.

So to work out how much of your earnings are due to people preferring your brand, the valuers have to:

- get the forecasted revenues and profits for the branded business;

- separate out the earnings the business makes into "tangible" and "intangible" ones (tangible means things like factories, equipment, etc., i.e. things you can touch);

- identify how much of the "intangible earnings" are generated by your brand as opposed to other intangibles such as patents, distribution agreements, etc.

Those are your brand earnings – and they can go up or down according to what you do in the market.

2 How secure is that brand demand?

People might prefer you, but do they "demand" and positively insist on you and are you available everywhere they could possibly want you so that they can always get you? Take banks. A lot of people use Barclays, some people might even like them, but there is little evidence that we've seen that says people love them and want to have their babies. Whereas, in the UK, First Direct, or in the USA, Umpqua Bank, have incredibly loyal customers who positively rave about their bank and, probably, at least would want to foster their children. So the chances are that security of demand for the Barclays brand is likely to be comparatively lower than that for First Direct

So, to work out how secure that brand demand is, valuers must:

- identify how strong the loyalty and affinity to your brand is with your customers;
- identify other factors that affect that demand, such as how available you are, how strong the marketplace is in which your brand operates, etc.;
- do some funky maths to identify a risk rate that you can apply to the earnings – the stronger the demand, the lower the risk and vice versa.

3 Work out the brand value

At its simplest, this means that the risk rate you have worked out for your brand's demand in point 2 is applied to the forecasted brand earnings identified in point 1. There's lots of fancy-dan financial thinking here but the key phrase to remember is that this is a "discounted cash earnings" method. Or a DCE, if you want to sound down and hip with the finance dudes. That simply means that the future money you think you will earn (cash flow) has to be discounted by a probability that you will not earn all of it. And then you add all the discounted cash flow projections for the next 5 to 10 years and get a net present value or NPV.

It's a bit like the time-value theory of money: you know, £1 today is worth more to you than £1 next year. In fact, the value of that £1 next year would probably be only 90p in today's money because prices will have gone up, etc., etc. So if I have £1 this year and the £1 promised to me next year then the NPV (i.e. if I could bring the value of what that £1 could buy me next year forward to this year) would be £1.90 (i.e. £1 = 90p).

In a similar way the £1 million a company forecasts to earn each year over the next five years from its brand is probably not 100 per cent secure, because lots of things can happen. But the stronger the demand for its brand is, the more of that £1 million it can expect to earn each year.

Why is BP worth more than Starbucks as a brand?

A frequent question asked by the average marketeer is: "How come in all these most valuable brand surveys, boring brands in technology and telecoms are worth more than exciting brands in groovy consumer space-o-sphere?" Well, the answer is simply this: there's more money to be made in oil than in coffee. It all starts with how much money you are making as a branded business in the first place. A petroleum business like BP probably makes around £2 billion a day, every day. A groovy brand like Starbucks might make £1 billion per year if it's lucky. Sure, demand among Starbucks' consumers for its brand might be higher than demand among BP's consumers for the BP brand, but all that means is that Starbucks can be more sure of making a higher percentage of £1 billion every year than BP can expect of its £700 billion. The Starbucks brand may be worth 80 per cent of £1 billion it makes a year and BP's may be worth 10 per cent of £700 billion. BP is still going to have the higher brand value (£). Simple maths that is.

Anyway, the comparison is meaningless because Starbucks has no intention of drilling for oil, refining it and selling it in its coffee shops – consumers don't demand that of it, and we aren't demanding BP go global with coffee.

At this point, some of you will – a little like us – say, "Sorry, my brain's full, can we go back to the logos and stuff?"; while others will say, "Umm … a sloppy exposition of the main issues around this vital topic, they have not even mentioned remuneration for capital employed in the business". Either way, you'll be pleased to know that we are stopping here and that we have included in the appendix on page 208 a couple of books that will go into this in great detail, so much so that you will be able to try your own brand valuation at home!

More important than the mechanics of the methodology is how the valuation is used. Over the years, brand valuation has been used by companies to transform their business in the following ways:

- To move the brand to the centre of the business and ensure alignment with all operations.
- To help divest businesses that, while they may be good, are not helpful in building the core brand.
- To improve financial reporting and show the true value of the businesses.

Many businesses have used it to help explain to everyone who works for and with them what a great brand they have and how valuable it is and why, therefore, on no account, should anyone f*** with the logo!

Don't panic.

The Hitchikers' Guide to the Galaxy

WHEN TO MESS WITH YOUR LOGO — DRASTIC MEASURES

*12

Hopefully you haven't jumped straight to this chapter. If you have, to borrow a phrase from Douglas Adams' *The Hitchhiker's Guide To The Galaxy*, "Don't panic". In fact, you're probably missing the point. Go and make yourself a nice cup of tea and read the earlier chapters. If you're convinced that the only option is to reinvent the whole thing from the ground up, then read on. This chapter is a quick guide on when to throw away the mould.

After all, there's no shame in changing things. Change is remorseless; without change there can be no progression. When it comes to your brand, there are often times to change what you have – if you have modified everything else and you find that your logo, colours, type or "visual identity" simply aren't fitting with your new brand, or maybe aren't working hard enough. But, brand traveller, beware the fiddlers, the tweakers and the change-monkeys that are hell-bent on creating a portfolio piece or simply don't know how to work with things that they themselves haven't created from scratch. Avoid the "not invented here" syndrome.

There are only three times (essentially) when you need to change your brand:

1 When what your brand stands for is no longer relevant to enough people in the market.

2 When something catastrophic has damaged your credibility, e.g. Arthur Andersen whose fraudulent sign-off of Big Corporate America accounts saw the firm collapse.

3 When you have been bought out by another company that
wants to achieve economies of scale, e.g. Wannadoo which was
rebranded Orange when France Telecom – Wannadoo's owners –
decided they wanted one brand name for Internet and mobile
communications worldwide.

But beware of the "wrong change" syndrome, which typically
happens when:

■ research is misleading – e.g. Babycham removing its famous deer
logo because they thought people considered it old-fashioned;
but consumers possibly thought the whole positioning of the
brand was old-fashioned and that the deer was charming. The
deer was later reinstated;

■ somebody new comes in and wants to take things in a
"different" direction (we're not going to give you an example of
that, but most people know what we mean!).

There are clever things you can do to ensure your brand is
refreshed.

French Connection went and FCUK'd its logo didn't it?

Why? Well, they wanted to stand out in an increasingly aggressive and competitive market. They wanted to show the brand
had an attitude. And they wanted to create buzz, get people
talking about the brand. Still, you have to be either brave or
desperate to do that.

But the interesting thing about the FCUK logo was that,
though it f***ed with the logo, it didn't f*** with the brand.
The aesthetics of French Connection were evolved, not

radically altered; the brand name remained French Connection. Its positioning was not changed; it didn't go up or down market all of a sudden. It just ensured it remained relevant to the changing fashion of its time.

Or take Marks & Spencer, our M&S, yes your M&S. This was a brand, which everyone basically loved, but fewer were finding reasons to buy. They launched new advertising campaigns, brought in new designers, refreshed their food offering, jazzed up their stores and created a new logo Your M&S. But still essentially its positioning remained unchanged – quality and value reinterpreted for the 21st century, not for the 1980s.

One of our favourite stories of recent years is Plymouth Gin. This was an ailing brand that was truly f***ed. It lay ignored and neglected by its owner who decided to sell it off. Along came an entrepreneur called John Murphy. Almost the God-father of Modern Branding, by the way, having established the first proper brand consultancy Interbrand in the 1970s. He visited the distillery where the brand was made, was captivated by the story behind the brand and bought it from Allied Domecq with a couple of other people. The brand repositioned as a premium drink available in top-notch drinking places, redesigned the logo, the bottle and the identity and built a campaignable story around its remarkable heritage as one of the world's few distinctive gins. One that the British Navy had taken wherever they went. When the BBC's *Food and Drink* programme gave it huge approval ratings and damned the mainstream brands like Gordon's Gin for not being strong enough, Murphy's boat was launched properly. Fast forward 10 years and he had sold the brand to the owners of Absolut Vodka for several times more than he had bought it.

The point here is it's OK to f*** with your logo if you are not really f***ing with your brand. Most people think that it's the positioning of the brand that's the problem but it's not, it's the promise or the personality of the brand that needs to be updated. If your positioning is the problem then basically your brand is f***ed because, remember, positioning means what you want to be famous for and that must be driven by an enduring need. So if the positioning is not working it means either the need was not as enduring as you thought or you are no longer able to be famous for it. In which case, sadly, your brand is f***ed and you need to reinvigorate it dramatically like Plymouth Gin. Or you should lay it gently to rest. Create a new brand and move on.

And that brings us to the final chapter and the most important lesson you can ever learn in brand building.

THE LAST LESSON IN BRAND BUILDING

*13

Sex sells.

Because it does.

We don't want to get all Sigmund Freud on you here but sex is used either directly or indirectly, aggressively in your face or subtly at the back of your mind, to sell anything from diet sodas to ice cream. And you get loads of free column inches in the press and pictures of your ads too if you are really sexy with it, cos newspapers know sex sells too.

Sex sells.
Because it does.

From the Cadbury Flake chocolate bar ads of the swinging 1960s to the Magnum ads of the naughty noughties, here are a few of our favourites.

Häagen-Dazs ice-cream;
Wonderbra;
Diet Coke;
Armani;
D&G;
Puma;
Castlemaine XXXX beer (ironically);
FCUK (ironically) – FCUK fashion.

Here's some homework: try typing into YouTube or Google the word "sex" and these brands:

The 1969 Cadbury Flake ad: http://uk.youtube.com/watch?v=wEhfxGGCDzY;

the 1980s/1990s Cadbury flake ads which got more and more on the money shots: http://uk.youtube.com/watch?v=DCLggnjbsqQ&feature=related;

Ellesse or "orgasm/tennis" campaigns: http://uk.youtube.com/watch?v=UTQinvFuX3M; (you try playing this one in the office!);

"for play": http://uk.youtube.com/watch?v=EWjMZDoq0E0;

Puma "bj" viral/unofficial ad: http://www.adrants.com/2003/03/puma-ads-not-for-the-squeamish.php;

D&G "bj" campaign: http://www.adrants.com/2006/08/dolce-gabbana-gives-head-nod-to-puma-blow.php;

Häagen-Dazs body heat/thermal commercial (how the brand launched in the UK, using thermal imaging of the couple "getting it on" *9 and half weeks* style);

Magnum ice cream and Eva Longoria. Work it out! http://uk.youtube.com/watch?v=Xiqq4jO-g2o;

Lynx deodorant/chocolate: http://uk.youtube.com/watch?v=lCZ-6y2UEfM;

Lynx dry/mermaids: http://uk.youtube.com/watch?v=DHZ2lxhM1eI;

Bacardi mojito ad: http://uk.youtube.com/ watch?v=5RFxGn6C6ak; pestle & mortar – just a tad of innuendo?

Bacardi made to mix (drinks become dancers/lovers): http://uk.youtube.com/watch?v=LI0x9Y6ZMDQ;

Bacardi heroes – holding out for male pin-up heroes (one for the ladies);

Bacardi cat: http://uk.youtube.com/watch?v= x47vAoY8Gs4; "Been out chasing birds again?";

Kylie/Agent Provocateur: Kylie in her pants on a mechanical rodeo machine .... hmmm http://uk.youtube.com/ verify_age?next_url=/ watch%3Fv%3DPj049hVtz6A';

Wonderbra: http://images.google.co.uk/images? num=20&hl=en&q=wonderbra%20ads&um=1&ie=U TF-8&sa=N&tab=wi and http://www.thecoolhunter. net/ads/WONDERBRA-AD/.

Or find your own. Type "sexy ad" into either Google or YouTube or simply get on a plane to Milan.

Done your homework then?

Here endeth the lesson in brands.

EPILOGUE

All the top tips in one place

If you're too bored or lazy to read the whole book, or if you've read it once and just want a reminder of the key tips, then here they are from all the chapters. (You may have to refer back to some chapters for fuller context.)

You can rip these pages out if you like and stick them in a folder marked "Read and Never Forget".

Chapter 1 Why you need to be on the brand wagon

Because brands make you lots of money. You need a brand because:

1 people (that includes you and us) believe they stand for something they value personally and so are prepared to pay more for them or to buy them repeatedly;

2 (therefore) you make more money with one than without one;

3 they legally protect your rights to make that money – they protect your idea not just your product and so stop other people making money at your expense;

4 they allow you to launch new products and services, etc. under that idea more cheaply (i.e. so you can make even more money);

5 they act as a "barrier to entry" to competition in your market (you could make a cola drink sure but are you really going to be able to take on Coca-Cola™?);

6 they help attract and retain people who want to work for you – who help you make money;

7 in order to make that money continuously, they force you to deliver consistently a differentiated promise of value to your customers;

8 chicks dig 'em and guys think they're cool.

Brands make all this money because they make it easy for people to:

- find you;

- recommend you;

- be loyal to you.

Chapter 2 So what is a brand?

Definition

Legally, a brand means a trademark, which distinguishes the goods or services of one supplier from another. In marketing terms, a brand means a specific promise of value, which the business must deliver to its customer. And there is even an economic definition now: a brand is a corporate asset that generates specific and protectable revenues.

But, in our opinion, a brand is best described as the sum of all the parts of a business, product or organisation. Everything you do, everything you say is captured in your trademark.

What are the six rules to building a brand?

1 Develop a strategy that is clear and easy to understand.

2 Create a simple brand architecture that links the different things you do in a way that makes sense to your customers.

3 Develop a distinctive brand identity that you can protect by law.

4 Ensure you have a consistent and iconic customer experience across your products, the places in which you sell them and the people that work for you.

5 Set up dedicated brand management and measurement structures and processes.

6 Don't f*** with the logo.

Remember the brand-building mantra:

> "If I stay true to my promise, I'll make money."

Chapter 3 What is brand strategy?

Strategy means having a plan so brand strategy just means the plan for the brand.

What is a good brand strategy?

A good brand strategy answers the following five questions simply and clearly:

1 What will we stand for?

A clear idea of who the brand is targeted at and what it offers to those customers that is different from competitors.

2 How many sub-brands do we need?

A clear idea of how many brands or sub-brands it will own (we call this brand architecture).

3 What will our brand identity be?

A clear brief for its name, logo, etc.

4 How are we going to deliver this?

What are the promises it will make across product, people, communications and environments and will they be delivered so that people believe it?

5 How will we know we've succeeded?

What will be the measures we will use to judge success?

Questions you should ask about your brand strategy

1 How is this strategy going to help me meet my business objectives?

Good answers:

- Everyone in your market is talking about x, this talks about y (Nike versus Adidas).
- There's nothing intrinsically new about this, it's the way we'll do it that's different (innocent smoothies).
- No one has ever put x and y together before (e.g. the movie *Alien: Jaws in space*).
- What is your primary objective beyond revenue? (Answering with a smart question can win some points!)

Bad answers:

- What do you mean, "business objectives"?
- There's nothing different, we'll make our business out of copying what everyone has done (possible brownie points for refreshing honesty).

2 Why is this relevant to my customers and future customers and the people who work here?

Good answer:

- Your target customers want x above everything else.

Bad answer:

- This is what your competitor is talking about.

3 Can you explain this strategy in words of approximately one syllable that a person of average intelligence can understand?

Good answer:

- Yes.

Bad answer:

- It's not that simple.

4 Give me examples of what exactly this strategy might mean (in real life) for my business. And do you really think we can do this?

Good answer:

- Here's what types of products we could develop.
- Here's what could be done in store, etc., etc.

Bad answer:

■ We can evolve the campaign over time.

5 Am I going to need a new strategy in five years' time?

Good answer:

■ No.

Bad answer:

■ Change is the only constant.

Chapter 4 **The house that brand built**

Simple rules to follow in developing your brand architecture

1 You can have as many products and services as you like but keep your brands down to a minimum.

2 Assume therefore that any new product or initiative can fit into your existing brand unless proven otherwise.

3 You put your brand on what people think you are famous for or what you want to be famous for, we'll call this "the source of value", and don't put it on anything else. This is why BMW-branded spare parts in the Mini work. Mini's source of value is the exciting, cool, chic runaround car, not the brilliant engineering inside. BMW's source of value is in the brilliant engineering; it is the "ultimate driving machine".

4 You use simple descriptive naming or alpha-numerics to give customers information to help them find precisely what they want from your brand.

Questions to ask in developing your architecture

1 Is this product or service something that fits what we want our brand to be famous for?
   If yes, go to question 2. If no, either abandon it or give it a different brand (go to naming and identity guidelines).

2 Are we the only people responsible for delivering this to customers, i.e. is there any third party involved who could affect the perceived quality of the experience?
   If no, go to question 3. If yes, go to naming and identity guidelines.

3 Is this (a) essentially the same product or service but in a new format, channel or a new audience but with the same needs (e.g. it's Ariel but in a tab form not a powder, it's Tesco but delivered to your door direct, it's Calvin Klein fragrance but for women not men, it's Gap but for kids)?

   Or (b) similar but with an ownable and unique feature or benefit or targeted at an audience with an additional need?

   If (a) go to question 4, if (b) create a sub-brand (go to naming and identity guidelines).

4 Having got this far, is this so risky and are we so inexperienced in this category that we could really f*** up our logo?
   If yes, create a sub-brand (go to naming and identity guidelines). If no, give it the simplest product descriptor possible and launch it under our brand.

Chapter 5 **Apples, Oranges, Blackberrys and other fruit**™

Law 1: Get yourself a good name

Rule 1 – Get a simple, short, creative idea

Rule 2 – Start thinking about the "feeling" of the brand early on

Rule 3 – Learn to be objective

Rule 4 – Follow what you believe in and don't worry about literal meaning

Rule 5: – Be inspired by other brands but don't copy

Rule 6 – Understand the areas in which your identity needs to operate

Rule 7 – Don't worry about "will it fax?"

Rule 8 – Ask yourself how long this identity should last

Rule 9 – Give people the tools to join in with, not just implement, the brand

Rule 10 – Be wary of visual clichés

Rule 11 – Never launch a "logo" and pretend it's a "brand"

Rule 12 – Let everyone else catch up and then evolve and keep evolving

Chapter 6 It's the experience, stupid!

Step 1 Ask yourself the following: who are your target customers and what do they most value? What is their current experience like?

Step 2 What promises can our brand make that would distinguish us credibly and delight our customers during the experience?

Step 3 What do we need to do to our processes, people and products to deliver these promises?

Step 4 Align your organisation with the promise.

Step 5 Communicate externally.

Step 6 Measure it!

Chapter 7 Too many opinions and not enough cheese sandwiches

1 Do research among your own staff first. They often know more than your customers can tell you about what's wrong or right, or what you should or should not do.

2 Do observational or "ethnographic" research before you do anything else.

The main questions you should ask a research agency when they are pitching to you are as follows:

1 Sample: How big? Who exactly? Why?

2 Time frame: How long and when will fieldwork take place? Why?

3 Structure: What topics? What questions? How many closed? What order? Always ask to see the protocol (interview guide, discussion guide or questionnaire).

4 Fieldwork: Who is conducting it? Where?

5 Data collection and reporting: Who and how?

6 Presentation of findings: How, who, when?

Above all, make sure you are absolutely clear on the following:

1 What precisely is the objective of your research?

2 How are you going to use the findings of the research?

3 In what format do you want the research to be reported?

Chapter 8 Call in the lawyers

1 Get your trademark lawyer to give you his/her advice from the start.

2 Choose the most distinctive brand name you can.

3 Registering the brand name is not enough; choose a distinctive logo, trade dress, packaging, etc.

4 Don't kid yourself that because you have slapped a TM on something, you have got trademark protection.

5 Aggressively protect your rights.

6 Stop people using your brand name as a proxy for the generic product.

7 If you've got the muscle, send people out to shops and bars and see if people are given a competitor's alternative when they have asked for your brand.

8 If you can't get someone for a direct trademark infringement, get them for passing off.

9 Be aware of the dangers of being seen as a big brand Nazi.

10 Look at all the other forms of intellectual property you have – patents, copyrights, designs and the terms of franchise or distribution agreements, etc. Manage them in a coordinated way. And use them.

Chapter 9 Bow ties, ponytails and lunch at The Ivy

1 Understand the different type of agency you need for each task.

2 Manage the pitch properly so you can choose the right one.

3 Understand and manage as a team the agencies you have chosen to get the best work out of them.

4 Understand and agree the key principles that will determine the success of a great campaign.

How to get the best out of the pitch

1 Be clear about what you want.

2 Be clear about who you want.

3 Have a process that maximises your chances of finding the right partner.

4 Be honest with an incumbent.

5 Make sure that your team is fully prepared.

How to get the best out of the agency's work

Here are some good tips:

1 How you treat each individual agency

(a) Be clear about the work/brief.

(b) The power of yes.

(c) Know when and how to say no.

(d) Keep rechecking everything with the agency. This includes the quality of the strategy, the (creative) idea and the execution.

(e) Agencies work best for clients whom they find rewarding and enjoyable.

2 How you understand them as a team

(a) Understand egos and politics.

(b) Don't be fooled by the "we're all part of a global network" sales pitch.

(c) Understand that the different types of agencies may not get on.

(d) Clarify roles and responsibilities and establish common goals and *esprit de corps*.

Understand and agree the principles that will make a great campaign

1 Be ruthlessly single-minded in your campaign message to your target audience.

2 Understand your target audience's 24/7 360 media consumption.

3 Connect everything.

4 Dial up and dial down.

5 Be bold and relentless.

Chapter 10 Standing out and standing on your competition

Our top five tips for standing out are as follows:

1 Embrace don't replace.

2 Don't stuff it down people's throats.

3 Be audacious.

4 Be better not just different.

5 Spare some change, buddy.

Chapter 11 How to measure brand performance

1 Get the forecasted revenues and profits for the branded business.

2 Separate out the earnings the business makes into "tangible" and "intangible" ones (tangible means things like factories, equipment, etc., i.e. things you can touch).

3 Identify how much of the "intangible earnings" are generated by your brand as opposed to other intangibles such as patents, distribution agreements, etc.

4 Identify how strong the loyalty and affinity to your brand is with your customers.

5 Identify other factors that affect that demand, such as how available you are, how strong the marketplace is in which your brand operates, etc.

6 Do some funky economics involving S-curves to identify a risk rate that you can apply to the earnings – the stronger the demand, the lower the risk and vice versa.

Chapter 12 When to f*** with your logo: drastic measures

1 When what your brand stands for is no longer relevant to enough people in the market, e.g. Formica, which is forever associated with a particularly 1970s' approach to interior decor.

2 When something catastrophic has damaged your credibility, e.g. Arthur Andersen whose fraudulent sign-off of Big Corporate America accounts saw the firm collapse.

3 When you have been bought out by another company that wants to achieve economies of scale, e.g. Wannadoo.

Chapter 13 The last lesson in brand building

Sex sells.

Appendix 1
The Lexicon of Brand[1]

All these brandy-wandy terms explained in plain English.

Above-the-line advertising (ATL) Highly visible, big old-fashioned advertising, e.g. TV, cinema, print or outdoor.

Attitude branding Using the core idea as an ideology or philosophy to drive the brand, e.g. the essence of easyJet is in the easy, not the jet.

Below-the-line advertising (BTL) Specific and targeted advertising, to smaller groups, using response devices, for example, direct mail or invitations to expos.

Brainstorm A facilitated working session where people are free to contribute random views to solving a problem, normally recorded on a whiteboard. This technique encourages people to think faster, objectively and without consequence. It is successfully used to generate naming and other strategy-based activities.

Brand A feeling or description of a thing: understood by the combination of tangible and intangible assets. Often epitomised by a logo, name, identity system or combination of these things. The application of a brand, the process of using and effecting the brand's performance and behaviour in the market. I brand; you brand; let's brand; we are branding.

Brand architecture The way a portfolio of brands is structured. This is normally the basis of the brand model. Spanning from a "monolithic" architecture where the brand name and identity is used for all products and services to "free-standing" architecture to where a

---

[1] Courtesy of WHAM, a brand consultancy.

brand or corporation may be offstage and each product or service has its own particular brand. It's the difference between central control and free expression.

Brand asset Sometimes used to describe the cash value of a brand element of a business. Coined by some marketeers as a flippant way of describing what the brand may "own" – by opinion (not necessarily trademark law) in the market. See Brand value.

Brand audit A collection and assessment of current materials and assets the brand currently has. Normally including a lot of photography and, if you're really lucky, long trips around the world to gather it.

Brand book A book explaining the brand idea and theory. It can assist and inform brand communication briefs and application. Often used in conjunction with brand guidelines.

Brand endorsement in brand architecture where one brand supports rather than co-brands another. Normally used to borrow values from a parent brand. FMCG brands that have broad and segmented portfolios use this technique a lot, e.g. Cadburys.

Brand equity A term invented by brand consultants to describe a positive feeling or association with a brand. Attributed to the identity or PR that provides an asset to the brand. It is normally applied in the context of reviewing the brand identity or valuing the brand.

Brand essence The purest and simplest way of expressing the brand idea. Brand boiled down to the jus. See also Brand idea.

Brand experience Mainly used by agencies to describe controlled environments such as retail or expos where the brand is brought to life and is interactive. This can also apply to products, communications or behaviours. Brand experience is essentially the cause of recognition, understanding and reputation. This can be controlled or passive.

Brand extension Where the brand is applied to a new product or service. The effectiveness of the brand extension depends how far the extension is pushed and how credible the brand is in that area. Also known as brand stretch. You could think about this in terms of what feels right for a brand rather than simply "permission". It feels right that a nachos brand might make a dip to go with its nachos. It also makes sense that auto brands may have credibility in both cars and bikes. It makes less sense that a food brand would venture into cosmetics (unless it was well known for cucumbers).

Brand guardianship The role of facilitating and looking after the brand. This can be a client side and/or agency side role. Brand consultancies use the implementation and reference of brand books, strategy and brand guidelines to enforce brand guardianship.

Brand guidelines An internal tool that explains how to use or apply a brand. This may include sections on strategy that give the background to the brand, along with any specific guidance on identity systems.

Brand idea The central driving idea of the brand. Often supported by vision, mission and values in traditional brand consultancy. Also known as the big idea.

Brand identity (BI) The combination of tangible communication assets normally protected by the owner. Traditionally comprising logo, symbol, typefaces, colours and tone of voice. This can be broken down further to visual and verbal identity, but only really for the convenience of internal departments.

Brand image Derived from a 1980s term to describe the brand from the perspective of the consumer. Where the identity is something controlled by the owner, image is decided by the user.

Brand model The strategy and architecture of a brand expressed as a schematic. Often used as shorthand for different types or approaches to branding, for example, "Virgin's Championing model".

Brand positioning The position a brand occupies in comparison to its competition within a market. Usually accompanied by at least one "two by two" matrix, positioning can be manipulated as a result of the branding process.

Brand proposition The offer and benefit of the brand or sub-brand to the customer in specific terms. For example, the proposition of a hypermarket may be based around maximum choice, the proposition of a mini-market may be based around maximum service. This is also sometimes referred to as the brand value proposition.

Brand stretch Americanised version of extension. See Brand extension.

Brand-to-life Tangible items that are created during launch or rollout.

Brand value How much more of a premium people are prepared to pay that can be attributed to the brand, normally calculated for the benefit of shareholders, taxation or financial assessment of intangible assets.

Brown/black goods Major household appliances that are hi-tech, usually for entertainment and traditionally black. For example television, hi-fi, CD player, DVD, camcorder.

Cannibalism When one brand in a portfolio creates false competition that benefits neither, effectively cancelling out the other. In M&A[2]: when similar brands overlap without an increase in sales. FMCG brands are the usual culprits, think of this as bad brand extension.

Co-brand Where two (or more) brands are used together for a common purpose. This may mean endorsement, supplier co-brands retail (e.g. Sony available at Dixons). Or it may be more collaborative and equal, fashion houses and sports shoes, e.g. Yoshi and Adidas or Sony Bravia and Sky HD.

Corporate identity (CI) Essentially the same as brand identity, although literally applied to a corporation. The difference between a corporate and brand identity is often semantic and really a question of mindset. You can charge more for a brand identity. However, for the purposes of our Lexicon, by implication, "corporate" must be less sophisticated than brand. As brand is not necessarily something you can control, the real difference is in the mindset of the owner. Somewhat unfashionable, even old-fashioned, but hey, still working well for VW, Audi, Mercedes ... (insert your favourite car badge here).

[2] Mergers and Acquisitions

Customer journey An industry term used to describe the consumer's typical areas of interaction with a brand; from awareness to purchase, to lifetime relationship.

Customer relationship management (CRM) Marketing and response based upon the tracking of customer behaviour, for example loyalty cards.

Demographics The vital statistics of a target group of people, enabling the study of characteristics.

Differentiation In brand positioning, the demonstration or acknowledgement of a positive difference in a brand. Sometimes not very much, but a little difference can make all the difference.

Differentiator A single characteristic that supports differentiation.

Disruptive branding Using the idea of differentiation but in the extreme and more deliberately. A brand model that deliberately disobeys the market status quo and consequently causes a disruption in the market. This used to be called lateral thinking, or is sometimes described as "zigging when others zag". For example, in a market where the status quo was about heritage and volume of alcohol, Absolut Vodka built a brand around the bottle as an icon of style and fashionability.

Fast-moving consumer goods (FMCG) Things that you can buy off the shelf, everyday purchases.

Focus group A collective of people put into a room, plied with sandwiches and beer to encourage honest free-thinking and discussion which is recorded and used for research. Sometimes to supply self-evident truths, occasionally to bring devastating insights. For example, if Mitsubishi had used naming focus groups they would never have created the "Starion" product name. Legend has it that this was in fact a mispronounced version of "Stallion". Not much luck for Mitsubishi either with Pajero which had to be changed in Spain where it means the word for onanist (look it up). See qualitative and quantitative research.

Freestanding brand A brand, product or service that has no obvious link in brand identity to any other brand within its portfolio. The opposite of a monolithic brand.

Hygiene factor A mandatory or given thing that is required to compete in a market, e.g. broadband is a hygiene factor for internet providers. It's the opposite of a USP.

Ideation A forced abbreviation of "idea-creation" (key word: forced). The same as a brainstorm, only where people spend the first five minutes discussing the meaning of "ideation".

Launch The first time a brand is introduced to the market. A "hard launch" is aggressive, where the brand is proactively launched and is normally accompanied by PR, marketing and advertising. A "soft launch" is when no attention is sought. This can be for internal purposes or before a hard launch.

Logo A symbol or trademark used to represent the brand.

Logotype A symbol or trademark constructed from type. The invention of the term "wordmarque" describes a logo constructed from bespoke letterforms, implying that a logotype has a full suite of letterforms from which other communication can be constructed.

Master brand, main brand or monolithic brand A brand that controls and defines all sub-brands, products and services. Examples are BMW, Gucci or Shell.

Mergers and acquisitions (M&A) The categorisation of companies being bought, acquired or merging: generating the need for a review of portfolio management.

Me-too brand When a brand copies the identity cues from a category leader. Traditionally seen mostly in FMCG, for example most other cola packaging will copy the colour, typography and style of Coca-Cola's brand.

Mission statement This is what you need to do to bring your vision to life. It's also probably a good sanity check to test the credibility or ambitiousness of your vision. Sometimes the mission and the vision are blurred, but a vision is future tense, mission is present tense.

Multi-brand strategy This refers to the number of brands owned by the same company that are sold in the same physical place. Cereals or chocolate companies often have a number of competing brands for sale together. As consumers become more aware but less concerned about this, the more acceptable it becomes. Now BMW is happy to have some multi-brand dealerships that house both BMW and Mini in close proximity. See also segmentation and brand architecture.

Namestorm A brainstorm with the specific objective of naming.

Own-brand Retailers' own brand or label products that compete against FMCG product brands.

Parent brand In brand architecture the root brand, or one that endorses a sub-brand.

Personality Attributes of the brand that affect its behaviour. These are often humanised and are used as part of the strategy and guidance of a brand.

Point of difference (POD) Marketing term meaning the same as unique selling proposition or USP.

Point of purchase (POP) Unnecessary alternative way of describing point of sale (POS).

Point of sale (POS) In-store communications that are placed near product lines or till-points.

Product brand Branding of an individual product that has its own specific rules. Where the product is made the hero or stand-alone brand, i.e. with more prominence than the parent or master brand, e.g. PlayStation.

Qualitative research Research designed to test particular or specific scenarios. Tending to be more personal, and to go deeper into a subject, for example interviews or focus groups.

Quantitative research This tends to be broader and more generalised, and tested in greater numbers. Polls or surveys are a good example.

Rollout How the branding programme is brought to bear on the market, including launch and post-launch. Typically assuming a cascading manner, the brand may be launched sequentially across different demographics, markets or countries.

Segmentation The division of the brand across specific demographic groups.

Share of mind A marketing phrase used to describe the measurement of understanding and recognition of a brand. Usually measured by consumer recall.

Share of wallet A marketing phrase more widely remembered by business, meaning the measure of purchasing frequency, i.e. how many people actually buy something.

Stand-alone brand See Freestanding brand.

Strapline; slogan or tagline A mnemonic device that articulates the brand proposition. The phrase you're intended to associate with the brand. For example, Nike's strapline is "Just do it".

Strategic initiatives Thoughts and decisions taken with an overall, longer-term view. Applied to communication means brand-led, i.e. things designed to build the reputation of the brand. Launches of brands are strategic rather than tactical. For example, "We believe in service, value and quality" is a strategic statement.

Sub-brand In brand architecture, a product brand that is governed by the parent brand. It may have its own specific rules within the main brand structure. For example, Ford Mondeo or Apple iPod.

T-shaped A broad and deep concept that could have its axis dynamics described as a "T".

Tactical initiatives Thoughts and decisions used for offer-based or specific communications. For example, "money off during this week" is a tactical promotion.

Three-letter abbreviation (TLA) Just to see if you're paying attention.

Through-the-line advertising (TTL) Somewhere between above-the-line and below-the-line.

Tone of voice (TOV) How the brand speaks to its audience, normally described in a humanised way. This can be a very powerful part of the brand and is dependent on what content the brand has to communicate, i.e. information or a dialogue. For example, tones: warm and friendly; authoritative; straightforward and challenging.

Umbrella brand A brand that covers other brands, products or services that are more or less related. Not to be confused with the likes of James Smith & Sons of New Oxford Street, makers of fine canes and umbrellas.

Unique selling proposition (USP) An advertising concept from the 1970s that describes a specific product benefit.

Value for money (VFM) A positioning term coined from consumer language, describing good value.

Values These are qualities that are important to the brand and effectively define its promise. Informing the vision and mission part of brand strategy.

Verbal identity Essentially the same as tone of voice. Informs strapline, naming and any guidance as to how the brand speaks, including headline length and any other specifics.

Vision This is really the brand's reason for being, or what businesses set out to try and do. It's future facing, hence your vision of how things would be. Visions are great when they are ambitious, but to make them worthwhile they need to be interesting for what you're doing and not generic. It's pointless to include "to be the No. 1" at what you do in the modern world, this only works for no-nonsense manufacturers. It's more interesting to do something better or try your own new way. For example, part of Walt Disney's pioneering vision was "to entertain" people, not to be the No. 1 cartoon brand for aspirational children.

Visual identity (VI) The part of an identity system that shows how the brand looks. Can cover logo, typefaces, colours, photography, etc.

White goods Major household appliances that are usually for domestic upkeep of the home and are traditionally white. For example, washing machine, dishwasher, cooker, refrigerator. See also Brown/black goods.

Workshop Misleading, as neither working nor shopping takes place. A formal session involving clients, where strategic concepts are discussed and formulated. Brainstorms were invented so that idea sessions could be held with power-tool brands, without either party getting confused.

X-brand "Made up" or anonymous, average or leader brand in a sector. Used in advertising as a comparison.

Zeitgeist The spirit of the times. Think Damien Hirst exemplifying British modern art in the 1990s or *Big Brother* summing up television in the noughties. By no means exclusively a branding term, but used frequently. Things sometimes sound more interesting in German.

Zombie brand A dormant or old brand that has been brought back to life.

Appendix 2
Forty-five classes of the Trade Marks Register

Class 1

Chemicals used in industry, science and photography, as well as in agriculture, horticulture and forestry; unprocessed artificial resins, unprocessed plastics; manures; fire extinguishing compositions; tempering and soldering preparations; chemical substances for preserving foodstuffs; tanning substances; adhesives used in industry. Explanatory note: this class includes mainly chemical products used in industry, science and agriculture, including those that go to the making of products belonging to other classes.

Class 2

Paints, varnishes, lacquers; preservatives against rust and against deterioration of wood; colourants; mordants; raw natural resins; metals in foil and powder form for painters, decorators, printers and artists. Explanatory note: this class includes mainly paints, colourants and preparations used for protection against corrosion.

Class 3

Bleaching preparations and other substances for laundry use; cleaning, polishing, scouring and abrasive preparations; soaps; perfumery, essential oils, cosmetics, hair lotions, dentifrices. Explanatory note: this class includes mainly cleaning preparations and toilet preparations.

Class 4

Industrial oils and greases; lubricants; dust absorbing, wetting and binding compositions; fuels (including motor spirit) and illuminants; candles, wicks. Explanatory note: this class includes mainly industrial oils and greases, fuels and illuminants.

Class 5

Pharmaceutical, veterinary and sanitary preparations; dietic substances adapted for medical use, food for babies; plasters, materials for dressings; material for filling teeth; dental wax; disinfectants; preparations for destroying vermin; fungicides, herbicides. Explanatory note: this class includes mainly pharmaceuticals and other preparations for medical purposes.

Class 6

Common metals and their alloys; metal building materials; transportable buildings of metal; materials of metal for railway tracks; non-electric cables and wires of common metal; ironmongery, small items of metal hardware; pipes and tubes of metal; safes; goods of common metals not included in other classes; ores. Explanatory note: this class includes mainly unwrought and partly wrought common metals as well as simple products made of them.

Class 7

Machines and machine tools; motors and engines (except for land vehicles); machine coupling and transmission components (except for land vehicles); agricultural implements; incubators for eggs. Explanatory note: this class includes mainly machines, machine tools, motors and engines.

Class 8

Hand tools and implements (hand operated); cutlery; side arms; razors. Explanatory note: this class includes mainly hand-operated implements used as tools in respective professions.

Class 9

Scientific, nautical, surveying, electric, photographic, cinematographic, optical, weighing, signalling, checking (supervision), lifesaving and teaching apparatus and instruments, apparatus for recording, transmission or reproduction of sound or images; magnetic data carriers, recording discs; automatic vending machines and mechanisms for coin-operated apparatus; cash registers, calculating machines, data-processing equipment and computers; fire extinguishing apparatus. Computer software supplied from the internet; electronic publications (downloadable) provided online from databases or the internet; computer software and telecommunications apparatus (including modems) to enable connection to databases and the internet; computer software to enable searching of data; digital music (downloadable) provided from the internet; digital music (downloadable) provided from MP3 internet websites.

Class 10

Surgical, medical, dental and veterinary apparatus and instruments, artificial limbs, eyes and teeth; orthopaedic articles; suture materials. Explanatory note: this class includes mainly medical apparatus, instruments and articles.

Class 11

Apparatus for lighting, heating, steam generating, cooking, refrigerating, drying, ventilating, water supply and sanitary purposes.

Class 12

Vehicles; apparatus for locomotion by land, air or water.

Class 13

Firearms; ammunition and projectiles; explosives; fireworks. Explanatory note: this class includes mainly firearms and pyrotechnical products.

Class 14

Precious metals and their alloys and goods in precious metals or coated therewith, not included in other classes; jewellery, precious stones; horological and chronometric instruments. Explanatory note: this class includes mainly precious metals, goods in precious metals and, in general, jewellery, clocks and watches.

Class 15

Musical instruments.

Class 16

Paper, cardboard and goods made from these materials, not included in other classes; printed matter; book-binding material, photographs; stationery; adhesives for stationery or household purposes; artists' materials; paint brushes; typewriters and office requisites (except furniture); instructional and teaching material (except apparatus); plastic materials for packaging (not included in other classes); playing cards; printer type; printing blocks. Explanatory note: this class includes mainly paper, goods made from that material and office requisites.

Class 17

Rubber, gutta-percha, gum, asbestos, mica and goods made from these materials and not included in other classes; plastics in extruded form for use in manufacture; packing, stopping and insulating materials; flexible non-metallic pipes. Explanatory note: this class includes mainly electrical, thermal and acoustic insulating materials and plastics, for use in manufacture in the form of sheets, blocks and rods.

Class 18

Leather and imitations of leather, and goods made of these materials and not included in other classes; animal skins, hides; trunks and travelling bags, umbrellas, parasols and walking sticks; whips, harness and saddlery. Explanatory note: this class includes mainly leather, leather imitations, travel goods not included in other classes and saddlery.

Class 19

Non-metallic building materials; non-metallic rigid pipes for building; asphalt, pitch and bitumen; non-metallic transportable buildings; non-metallic monuments. Explanatory note: this class includes mainly non-metallic building materials.

Class 20

Furniture, mirrors, picture frames; articles made of wood, cork, reed, cane, wicker, horn, bone, ivory, whalebone, shell, amber, mother-of-pearl, meerschaum, and substitutes for all these materials, or plastics which are not included in other classes. Explanatory note: this class includes mainly furniture and its parts and plastic goods, not included in other classes.

Class 21

Household or kitchen utensils and containers (not of precious metal or coated therewith); combs and sponges; brushes (except paint brushes); brush-making materials; articles for cleaning purposes; steel wool; unworked or semi-worked glass (except glass used in buildings); glassware, porcelain and earthenware not included in other classes. Explanatory note: this class includes mainly small, hand-operated utensils, glassware and articles in porcelain.

Class 22

Ropes, string, nets, tents, awnings, tarpaulins, sails, sacks and bags (not included in other classes); padding and stuffing materials (except rubber or plastics), raw fibrous textile materials. Explanatory note: this class includes mainly rope and sail manufacture products, padding and stuffing materials and raw fibrous textile materials.

Class 23

Yarns and threads, for textile use.

Class 24

Textiles and textile goods, not included in other classes; bed and table covers. Explanatory note: this class includes mainly textiles (piece goods) and textile covers for household use.

Class 25

Clothing, footwear, headgear.

Class 26

Lace and embroidery, ribbons and braid; buttons, hooks and eyes, pins and needles; artificial flowers.

Class 27

Carpets, rugs, mats and matting, linoleum and other materials for covering existing floors; wall hangings (non-textile). Explanatory note: this class includes mainly products intended to be added as furnishings to previously constructed floors and walls.

Class 28

Games and playthings; gymnastic and sporting articles not included in other classes; decorations for Christmas trees.

Class 29

Meat, fish, poultry and game; meat extracts; preserved, dried and cooked fruits and vegetables and other comestibles.

Class 30

Coffee, tea, cocoa, sugar, rice, tapioca, sago, artificial coffee; flour and preparations made from cereals, bread, pastry and confectionery, ices; honey, treacle; yeast, baking-powder, salt, mustard; vinegar, sauces (condiments); spices, ice. Explanatory note: this class includes mainly foodstuffs of plant origin prepared for consumption or conservation as well as auxiliaries intended for the improvement of the flavour of food.

Class 31

Agricultural, horticultural and forestry products and grains not included in other classes; live animals; fresh fruits and vegetables; seeds, natural plants and flowers; foodstuffs for animals, malt. Explanatory note: this class includes mainly land products not having been subjected to any form of preparation for consumption; live animals and plants as well as foodstuffs for animals.

Class 32

Beers; mineral and aerated waters and other non-alcoholic drinks, fruit drinks and fruit juices; syrups and other preparations for making beverages. Explanatory note: this class includes mainly non-alcoholic beverages, as well as beer.

Class 33

Alcoholic beverages (except beers).

Class 34

Tobacco; smokers' articles; matches.

Class 35

Advertising, business management; business administration; office functions; retail services; mail order services; online retail services. Advertising and promotion services and information services relating thereto; business information services; all provided online from a computer database or the Internet; compilation of advertisements for use as Web pages on the Internet; completion of directories for publishing on the Internet, provision of space on websites for advertising goods and services; auctioneering provided on the Internet; business administration services for the processing of sales made on the Internet. Explanatory note: this class includes services rendered mainly by persons or organisations principally with the object of:

1 help in the working or management of a commercial undertaking;

2 or help in the management of the business affairs or commercial functions of an industrial or commercial enterprise, as well as

services rendered by advertising establishments primarily undertaking communications to the public, declarations or announcements by all means of diffusion and concerning all kinds of goods or services.

Class 36

Insurance; financial affairs; monetary affairs; real-estate affairs; information services relating to finance and insurance, provided online from a computer database or the Internet; home banking; Internet banking. Explanatory note: this class includes services rendered mainly in financial and monetary affairs and services rendered in relation to insurance contracts of all kinds.

Class 37

Building construction; repair; installation services; information services relating to repair or installation, provided online from a computer database or the Internet; installation and repair of telecommunications apparatus; installation and repair of computer hardware. Explanatory note: this class includes services rendered mainly by contractors or sub-contractors in the construction or making of permanent buildings, as well as services rendered by persons or organisations engaged in the restoration of objects to their original condition or in their preservation without altering their physical or chemical properties.

Class 38

Telecommunications; telecommunication of information (including Web pages), computer programs and any other data; electronic mail services; providing user access to the Internet (service providers); providing telecommunications connections to the Internet or databases;

providing access to digital music websites on the Internet; providing access to MP3 websites on the Internet; delivery of digital music by telecommunications; operating search engines. Explanatory note: this class includes mainly services allowing at least one person to communicate with another by sensory means. Such services include those that:

1 allow a person to talk to another;

2 transmit messages from one person to another; and

3 place a person in oral or visual communication with another (radio and television).

Class 39

Transport, packaging and storage of goods; travel arrangement and information, including provided online from a computer database or the Internet. Explanatory note: this class includes services rendered mainly in transporting people or goods from one place to another (by rail, road, water, air or pipeline) and services necessarily connected with such transport, as well as services relating to the storage of goods in a warehouse or other building for their preservation or guarding.

Class 40

Treatment of materials; information services relating to treatment of materials, provided online from a computer database or the Internet. Explanatory note: this class mainly includes services not included in other classes, rendered by the mechanical or chemical processing or transformation of objects or inorganic substances. For the purposes of classification, the mark is considered a service mark only in cases where processing or transformation is affected for the account of another person. A mark is considered a trademark in all cases where the substance or object is marketed by the person who processed or transformed it.

Class 41

Education; provision of training; entertainment; sporting and cultural activities; publishing services, information relating to entertainment or education, provided online from a computer database or the Internet; electronic games services provided by means of the Internet; providing online electronic publications (not downloadable); publication of electronic books and journals online; operating chat rooms; providing digital music (not downloadable) from the Internet; providing digital music (not downloadable) from MP3 Internet websites.

Class 42

Scientific and technological services and research and design relating thereto; industrial analysis and research services; design and development of computer hardware and software; legal services.

Class 43

Services for providing food and drink; temporary accommodation.

Class 44

Medical services; veterinary services; hygienic and beauty care for human beings or animals; agriculture, horticulture and forestry services.

Class 45

Personal and social services rendered by others to meet the needs of individuals; security services for the protection of property or individuals.

Appendix 3
Vague but clever things to say about brands

Things that you should know so you don't feel intimidated at the agency Christmas party

And so the Sistine Chapel brief gag may have been true after all – maybe the Mona Lisa's smile is actually a client secretly knowing that she will change the colour of this next week anyway ...

Done it already, mate. Worked on a similar job in Asia back in the 1960s (or 1970s, or 1980s or 1990s or last year), depending on your age.

Brands differ from corporations because they deliberately stand for something.

If enough people think the same thing about a thing, that's its brand.

Don't confuse great brands with great identities.

Unless you are the cool dude who designed the NASA logo, branding isn't rocket science.

The dot.com lesson: if the idea is good enough to make a shop from, then make it a dot.com.

All businesses need brands – but does the market really need your business?

If Newton had an iPod fall on his head, would have he invented branding?

Just as Galileo (and Copernicus before him) realised that the earth was not the centre of the universe, so too do we acknowledge that a logo is not the centre of a brand.

In the same way that man creates God – and most things – in his own image, so he does with brand identity.

If you're a brand creator, sometimes you have to make a lot of dead cows before you find your dead shark.

Appendix 4
A few books on branding we like

Brands and Branding

Naming

The Brand Gap

Trademarks

Brands: The World's New Wealth Creators

The 22 Laws of Branding

Appendix 5
How to make a great cup of tea

Boil kettle

Scald pot with a little water

Put one teabag or teaspoon of tea per person plus "one for the pot"

Brew for three minutes

Pour into cup

Add milk and sugar to taste

Drink with a biscuit or a nice piece of cake

Appendix 6
Good recipes

Our book wouldn't be complete without some bonus recipes.

Three-cow stew anyone?

JON – "WHERE'VE THE RECIPES GONE!? ;-)"

ANDY – "SORRY, JON, I LEFT THEM ON THE PLANE ALONG WITH MY COMPUTER THAT'S GOT THE PRESENTATION ON IT"

Index